W9-ADF-602

For the INDEPENDENT PEACEFUL REUNIFICATION OF KOREA

Kim Il Sung

KIM IL SUNG

For the
INDEPENDENT
PEACEFUL
REUNIFICATION
of KOREA

INTERNATIONAL
PUBLISHERS

Copyright © 1975 by International Publishers Co., Inc.
All Rights Reserved

Printed in the United States of America

Library of Congress Cataloging in Publication Data

Kim, Il-song, 1912-
For the independent, peaceful reunification of Korea.

Selections from the author's writings, speeches, and reports, 1948-1974.
1. Korean reunification question (1949-   ) —
Addresses, essays, lectures. I. Title.
DS917.K5517813   320.9′519′04   75-9985
ISBN 0-7178-0426-7
ISBN 0-7178-0427-5 pbk.

Publisher's Note

These selections from the works of President Kim Il Sung, the great leader of the Korean people and prominent world Communist leader, are more than just of historical interest to U.S. readers. The urgency of their message deeply involves the American Korean people.

For three decades U.S. troops have occupied south Korea, fostering and maintaining an artificial division of the country. This split has brought the Korean people enormous suffering and innumerable personal tragedies. Today, even the most elementary rights of mutual visits and exchange of mail between families and friends in north and south Korea are absent. Millions of people in both parts of the country have no knowledge as to the whereabouts of relatives and close friends, and whether they are dead or alive. The fact that new generations of Korean youth are growing up in a divided land only deepens the inherent tragedy.

The documents collected in this book demonstrate that the President of the Democratic People's Republic of Korea, from the very first days of this division, advanced reasonable, practical and principled proposals to unite the Korean people. The reader will see their exceptional merit in the fundamental fact that whatever the shape of the proposals made, they were, and are, designed to permit the Korean people, democratically and without outside interference, to peacefully solve for themselves the question of reunification.

In the years, which followed the great victory over fascism in World War II, irresistible winds of change, among them the desire of hundreds of millions of people for national liberation in Asia, Africa and Latin America, swept through the world.

Yet from the first days in September 1945, U.S. government policy toward Korea has been aggressive, imperialist, unjust. In 1950, to thwart the unanimous will of the Korean people for a united nation, the U.S. armed forces unleashed a holocaust in

Korea. When the flames of this terrible war subsided, every city and village in the north was destroyed and millions of men, women and children were murdered and mutilated, along with hundreds of thousands of American youth.

Since the 1953 armistice which ended the U.S. aggression, the U.S. government has maintained more than 40,000 soldiers and nuclear forces in south Korea. This enormous burden for the Korean and American people, is maintained despite the fact that the armistice calls for complete withdrawal of foreign troops and reunification of the country. Moreover, in direct violation of the 1953 agreements, the U.S. signed a "treaty" with its own creation, the tyrannical regime in the south, extending foreign occupation interminably.

The U.S. government declares that its policy is concerned with the freedom of the Korean people! This hypocrisy is bared by the martial law imposed upon the people of south Korea. The military dictatorship of Park Chung Hee cruelly represses every attempt to wipe out extreme corruption and exploitation and to end foreign domination of the country. Nevertheless, the demand for reunification, for a more just political and social system grows stronger. How long can a surging national liberation movement be smothered without recourse to renewed U.S. warfare? The great danger is that Park and other U.S. puppets, with CIA connivance, will precipitate a new war in order to thwart the unanimous will of Korean people for unity. It is this great danger for both peoples, for world peace, that gives President Kim Il Sung's proposals their forcefulness and urgency.

The just proposals placed forth by President Kim Il Sung have the staunch support of the overwhelming majority of governments, statesmen and peoples throughout the world. In our own country, increasing numbers of Senators and Congressmen, influential people in and outside of government, recognize the need to bring this dubious U.S. policy to an end. We have neither the right nor the need to perpetuate the colonial status of south Korea. It is time to withdraw all our troops and rearrange our relations with all of Korea on a peaceful, mutually beneficial basis. These writings of President Kim Il Sung are a major contribution toward that noble end.

September 9, 1975

Contents

Against the Election of a Reactionary Separate Government in South Korea and for the Achievement of Korea's Reunification and Independence

Speech Made at the 25th Meeting of the Central Committee of the Democratic National United Front of North Korea, March 9, 1948

Friends, due to the pressure from the U.S. government the "UN Little Assembly" adopted a resolution in February on holding a separate election in south Korea for the so-called "national government of Korea."

The resolution of the "UN Little Assembly" is a reprint of the U.S. resolution submitted by U.S. Secretary of State Marshall.

According to the resolution the election for a separate government in south Korea will be held under the supervision of the "UN Commission on Korea" and the election regulations will become effective only when Lieutenant General Hodge, U.S. army commander in south Korea, approves them.

This illegal resolution serves the aggressive policy of U.S. imperialists who wantonly trample on the sovereignty of the Korean people and try to perpetuate the division of our country.

The resolution, which is opposed to the reunification and independence of Korea along democratic lines, completely runs counter to our people's national interests.

Therefore, this undemocratic resolution the U.S. imperialists and their followers had concocted could not but evoke a massive indignation from all the people in north and south Korea and meet with the strongest resistance of the people who opposed the sinister trickery of the U.S. imperialists and their lackeys— pro-U.S. and pro-Japanese elements, traitors to the nation and all the other reactionary elements.

1. Who has Frustrated the Implementation of the Decision of the Moscow Conference on the Establishment of a Unified Democratic Government of Korea and How?

The decision adopted at the Moscow Conference of Foreign Ministers of the Soviet Union, the United States and Britain on the 27th of December, 1945 opened up the road to the correct solution of the Korean question.

The conference deemed it necessary to establish a provisional democratic government of Korea in order to "create conditions for restoring Korea as an independent state, ensuring her development on a democratic principle and doing away quickly with the evil aftereffects of the long Japanese rule."

The entire Korean people gave full support to the decision of the Moscow three ministers conference and demonstrated their attitude internally and externally at mass meetings held in all parts of the country. All the truly democratic political parties and social organizations in north and south Korea declared themselves for the decision.

Only the handful of reactionary political parties and their quislingite heads came out against it with the active support of the U.S. military government in south Korea. These reactionary elements still remain faithful lackeys of the U.S. imperialists who do not want Korea to develop as a free and independent country.

The U.S. policy of subjugating Korea was brought to full light already at the time of the Moscow conference. As everyone knows, the U.S. government insisted at that time that Korea be put under trusteeship.

According to the U.S. imperialists' plan Korea would have to be "administered" by a supreme commissioner who would act in the name of an administrative organ composed of representatives of the Soviet Union, the United States, Britain and China. The plan envisaged this "administration" of Korea for five years and, if necessary, for another five years. It would not be until this period was over, the U.S. proposal said, that the period of guardianship would begin, and the establishment of a Korean government was not mentioned at all in the proposal.

The Soviet side opposed the U.S. proposal and suggested the establishment of a provisional democratic Korean government. It maintained that measures be taken, with the participation of the provisional government, to assist in the Korean people's political, economic and social progress and the democratic development of Korea and in the establishment of an independent state.

It was this Soviet proposal that was adopted in substance at the Moscow conference.

Friends, I remind you of this fact because a better understanding of the recent events which will affect our country's future calls for the clarification of the fact that from the beginning there were two lines for the solution of the Korean question which were contrary to each other in principle.

For two years the U.S. imperialists openly neglected to carry out the decision of the Moscow three ministers conference which they had signed. The whole course of the work of the U.S.S.R.-U.S. Joint Commission convinced the Korean people more clearly that the commitments given by the U.S. government at the Moscow conference were nothing but a fraud.

Both sides had to agree to set up a democratic government of Korea, but the U.S. delegates contradicted the adopted decision all the time and clung to their incorrect view that the only way to establish a unified government was to set up a reactionary government in an undemocratic way, a government in which the stooges of U.S. imperialism would have the upper hand. The U.S. imperialists not only refused to lend an ear to the opinion of the popular masses of Korea, but have suppressed more cruelly the democratic political parties and social organizations in south Korea. In south Korea, which is occupied by the U.S. army troops, the democratic political parties and social organizations are disbanded or find themselves forced to go underground.

This is how the decision of the Moscow three ministers conference on the establishment of a unified provisional democratic government of Korea has fallen through. This is how the U.S. imperialists delayed and wrecked the work of the U.S.S.R.-U.S. Joint Commission.

In order to remove the obstacles which hindered and delayed the building of a completely independent and sovereign state of the Korean people, the Soviet delegate made a new suggestion, which is as follows: "The Soviet Union always had and has a regard for peoples of smaller states and fought and is fighting for their independence and sovereignty. The Soviet delegation, therefore, believes that only when the Soviet and the U.S. troops have been withdrawn from Korea can the Korean people be provided with the opportunity of establishing a government for themselves without the aid and participation of the Allied Powers. The Soviet delegation declares that the Soviet army is prepared to withdraw from Korea simultaneously with the U.S. troops, on condition that the U.S. delegation agrees to our proposal for the withdrawal of all the foreign troops in early 1948." The entire Korean people enthusiastically supported this fair proposal which offered a possibility for settling the Korean issue in a most correct and smooth way.

But the United States rejected this just proposal of the Soviet Union. Having frustrated the implementation of the decision of the Moscow conference, the U.S. government put the Korean question to the UN General Assembly debate without any justifiable reason.

The Yanks have the nasty habit of breaking their promise when the circumstances are unfavorable for them. This is not the first time they are false to their word. On the German question, too, they are acting in violation of the Potsdam Agreements they signed. The Korean people clearly know that the

U.S. imperialists aim at nullifying the decision of the Moscow conference by hook or by crook and rejecting the Soviet proposal on the simultaneous withdrawal of the Soviet and U.S. troops from Korea.

All these facts thoroughly expose the sinister design of the U.S. government which does not want the building of a unified independent state in Korea.

2. U.S. Imperialism and the Korean Question in the United Nations

It is a common knowledge that the just proposal of the Soviet delegation to invite representatives of the Korean people to the United Nations to participate in the discussion of the Korean question, was turned down because of the obstructive manoeuvres of the U.S. delegation.

There have been debates in the United Nations about the future of many nations, but the Korean question was the first to be discussed without the attendance of representatives of the nation concerned. The United States barred the UN General Assembly from hearing the Korean people's will. Consequently, the "resolution" on the Korean question was adopted at will without the participation of the Korean people's representatives.

What is this if not an act of attempting to deceive the Korean people? What is this if not an act of disregard and insult to our nation?

Why did the United States oppose the attendance of the Korean people's representatives at the UN General Assembly session? Because the United States was afraid of exposure to the world of the actual conditions in south Korea, a lawless land where the police and terrorist groups run rampant under the rule of the U.S. military government.

In the two and a half years of U.S. imperialist rule no dmeocratic reform has been carried out in south Korea. The south Korean people are now suffering from hunger and poverty. Owing to inflation and mass unemployment the working people's living conditions have become unbearable.

The U.S. imperialist aggressors are encouraging in every way the activities of the handful of reactionary elements in south Korea who have been discarded by the Korean people. They openly abet and take under their wings the terrorist activities of the fascist organizations which oppose the democratic forces of south Korea and murder noted activists of the democratic political parties and social organizations. This policy of the U.S. military government is arousing an irrepressible indignation among the entire Korean people.

In its letters of last October to the Soviet and U.S. governments, the Central Committee of the Democratic National United Front of North Korea referred to these facts, saying, "We already well know that in south Korea where the U.S. army troops are stationed the democratic freedom of the people is restricted, the democratic political parties and social organizations suppressed and their leaders arrested and imprisoned under various pretexts."

Afraid of the Korean people's voice, the U.S. delegation was dead set against the attendance of our people's representatives at the debates on the Korean question by the UN General Assembly.

The resolution of the Soviet delegation which proposed to the Soviet and U.S. governments to withdraw their troops from north and south Korea simultaneously and leave the problem of establishing a unified democratic government to the Korean people themselves, was objected to by the UN General Assembly owing to the underhand manoeuvres of the United States.

The delegations of Ukraine, Czechoslovakia, Poland and many other democratic countries fully supported the proposal of the Soviet delegation for the withdrawal of foreign troops from Korea and strongly asserted, "Now, there is no ground whatsoever for continuing with the occupation policy in Korea and it is an absolute necessity to get the foreign troops withdrawn from Korea in order to prevent foreign interference in the future election for a government."

This just stand of our friends, who sincerely want our people to attain freedom and independence, could not but alarm the U.S. imperialists.

The U.S. delegation did everything to bring pressure to bear upon those countries which were subordinated politically and economically to the United States and set into motion their voting machine, so that the proposal for the withdrawal of foreign troops from Korea was rejected and the resolution on the creation of the so-called "UN Temporary Commission on Korea" was railroaded through.

Our people are well aware that the mission of this "Commission" is to cover up the colonial enslavement policy of the U.S. imperialists in Korea.

The suggestion that elections be held under conditions where there is undisguised foreign interference in our country's internal affairs is tantamount to proposing to elect as members of the government those who are relying on the U.S. military government, that is, traitors to the nation who value the interests of their foreign patrons and themselves more than the future of their nation.

Friends, the creation of the "UN Commission on Korea" is unfair and runs counter to the principle of self-determination of nations, and so it is impermissible. The "UN Commission on Korea" is a puppet organization and it has neither ability nor authority to solve the Korean question.

It is only natural that the "UN Commssion on Korea," upon arrival in Seoul, should have met with waves of national indignation from the people not only in north Korea but also in south Korea.

The south Korean reactionaries, and their patrons, the U.S. imperialists, used every artifice to give a false impression that public opinion favored the work of the "UN Commission on Korea," but their attempt came to nothing.

The people were decidedly against the entry into Seoul of the "UN Commission on Korea." The masses of the south Korean workers, peasants and intellectuals declared strikes and held demonstrations in determined opposition to the latest trickery of U.S. imperialism against Korea.

The U.S. military government in south Korea stopped food rationing to the strikers in an attempt to dampen the fighting spirit of the people. At the same time, the U.S. military government and the south Korean police arrested a large number of democratic personages. According to the watered-down data released by them, more than 400 persons were apprehended on the very day when the "UN Commission on Korea" arrived in Seoul.

According to the newspaper *Tongrip Sinbo* of January 30 this year the Peasants' Union of South Korea sent a letter to the "UN Commission on Korea," saying, "The Korean people are now well aware that the way to democracy and independence, through the establishment of a unified north-south government for which they long, lies solely in assuring, through the immediate withdrawal of the two armies, the formation of their government for themselves free from interference by these armies. . . .

"We are categorically against your activities to implement the so-called UN resolution. On behalf of the 14 million farming population of south Korea, we hereby strongly demand that you quit this land. We declare that, together with all the other sections of the people, we will defend this land against all imperialist aggression even if it may cost our lives and will fight till we win independence and sovereignty for the whole of the north and the south."

The Democratic Women's Union of South Korea stated, "We will categorically reject any kind of elections other than an independent and free election with no foreign interference, to be held after the withdrawal of the two armies. The Koreans, even children, know that the UN resolution retards the settlement of the Korean question and only brings about territorial partition, national division, delay in the withdrawal of foreign troops and subordination which the Korean people are dead set against. . . .

"With all the Korean women and all other people, we strongly demand that the foreign troops withdraw at once and thus leave the establishment of a government in the hands of the people. The people will fight to the end for complete independence."

The Democratic Patriotic Youth League of South Korea, the Federation of Korean Residents In Japan and many other organizations, too, issued statements strongly opposing the resolution of the UN General Assembly on Korea.

According to the *AP* the U.S. army troops have frenziedly reinforced their armament in order to cope with all the south Korean people's protests and demonstrations against the "UN Commission on Korea." Some 100 patriots were killed in clashes between the police and the demonstrators.

As you see, the U.S. military government authorities and the reactionary elements in south Korea are preparing to hold an "election" for a "government" by force of arms.

The Korean people's struggle against the interference of the U.S. imperialists in the internal affairs of their country got the "UN Commission on Korea" into a great scrap. So the U.S. imperialists framed another plot and forced the "UN Little Assembly" to adopt an unwarrantable resolution again.

Pressured by the United States, the "UN Little Assembly" decided to hold a separate election in south Korea. Using the "UN Little Assembly," the United States is following the policy of dividing our country and pursuing its aggressive ends.

Thus, there are now two different lines for settling the Korean question which make a strong contrast with each other.

The U.S. line is an aggressive one designed to divide Korea artificially, establish a reactionary government congenial to the United States in the name of the United Nations, and turn south Korea into a complete colony.

The Soviet line is a just one which truly makes for Korea's freedom and independence; and it is a line to make all the foreign troops withdraw from Korea as soon as possible, ensure the reunification of our country and establish a truly democratic unified government in Korea.

All the Korean people wholeheartedly support the latter.

3. Korea Will Become a Unified, Democratic Independent State

Friends, the first reaction to the decision of the "UN Little Assembly," which completely runs counter to our national interests, shows that the Korean people will never recognize nor approve a puppet government which will be set up under the patronage of the "UN Commission on Korea."

The decision of the "UN Little Assembly," cooked up by the

U.S. imperialists, is only favourable to the Syngman Rhee and Kim Song Su clique, a handful of traitorous reactionaries who betray the interests of the country and the people, and faithfully serve their foreing masters.

Noteworthy is the fact that voices are raised even in the right-wing camp against the U.S. imperialists, who are hindering our nation's reunification and independence under the signboard of the "UN Commission on Korea." The speech of Kim Won Yong, a former member of the so-called "Legislature" of south Korea, at a recent interview with U.S. pressmen is a graphic illustration of this. He severely criticized the U.S. military government in south Korea, and said that the United States "has turned south Korea into a police state," and that "the United States is forfeiting the Korean people's confidence." And he added, "The United Nations must not hold an election in south Korea now, for it cannot be an aboveboard or free election whatever form it may take."

An "election" of this kind, to be held under outrageous foreign interference, will result in the yielding of power to an insignificant number of ultra-right reactionary elements.

The reactionary elements in south Korea do not grant the people the slightest right to express their will. Syngman Rhee is thus manoeuvering to establish a fascist dictatorship in south Korea.

Even the reactionary publications in the United States have long made no secret of its designs on Korea. The Hearst paper *New York Journal and American* can be taken as an example. Quoting an authentic report obtained from the U.S. State Department, the paper said that the real intentions of certain quarters in the United States were "to establish a Republic of South Korea which will have the U.S. backing in its efforts to seize as soon as possible the half of Korea north of the 38th parallel." As you see, the intentions of the United States are to divide Korea, repress our people's desire for freedom and independence, insult our nation, and put a yoke of colonial slavery on our people again.

But the U.S. imperialists' intentions are one thing and the possibility of their realization is quite another. The 30 million

Korean people, who suffered for a long time under the colonial oppression of Japanese imperialism, never again want to become slaves who have no state to claim as their own. The people in north Korea who have truly won democratic rights and liberties and are directly benefiting from the agrarian reform, nationalization of industries, labor law and the equality of the sexes and from other democratic reforms, will never surrender the liberties and rights they have won.

One cannot reverse the wheels of history. Our fellow countrymen in south Korea, who are starving and maltreated, have already seen through the underlying motive of the U.S. imperialists in their disguise, and clearly perceived the true nature of their aggressive policy towards Korea.

The Korean people do not recognize the "UN Commission on Korea," which was organized in the absence of their representatives and in disregard of their will and interests.

Staging an "election" farce, the U.S. and Korean reactionary elements are now attempting to set up a "government" with the reactionary elements who toe the U.S. imperialist line. How the "free election" will be conducted can easily be foreseen from the mere fact that all the south Korean police have been now mobilized to hold this "election in an organized manner." The U.S. military government is preparing to use the vicious means which they used in suppressing democratic elections in other countries.

There is only one road which leads to out nation's regeneration, and that is the road of democratic development. Our demand remains unchanged. We demand that an all-Korea supreme legislative organ be elected on the principle of universal, direct and equal suffrage by secret ballot. The true people's supreme legislative organ thus elected should approve the constitution and establish a truly democratic people's government which will ensure the prosperity and development of the country and lead the people to happiness. All this is possible only when all the foreign troops withdraw simultaneously from Korea.

I appeal to all the Korean people, all the democratic forces and all the patriotic figures who long for our country's freedom and independence, to do all they can to frustrate the underhand design of the enemy to divide our country and enslave our people once again.

I appeal to all the patriotic and democratic forces to unite more firmly in the struggle for our country's freedom and independence.

Fellow countrymen, let's rise up against imperialist aggression which impedes our nation's reunification and infringes on our country's independence and sovereignty.

Let's thoroughly expose the reactionary elements and traitors to the nation who sell out our country to the U.S. imperialists.

Let's not be a party to the "election" farce and let's vigorously conduct a campaign to reject the "election."

Korean patriots, unite more firmly and bravely, come out in the struggle for the country's reunification, freedom and independence.

Long live a unified, free and democratic Korea!

The Korean People's Struggle for the Building of a Unified, Democratic Independent State

May 1950

1

Nearly five years have elapsed since our country was liberated from the protracted colonial oppression of Japanese imperialism and a broad avenue was opened up before our people for the building of a democratic and independent state. Korea is now a free country and for the first time the Korean people established their government on their land.

Immediately after liberation local people's committees were formed in all parts of Korea. The people's committees, formed with representatives of the workers, peasants, men in the cultural field, small tradesmen, entrepreneurs and people of various other strata, were a genuinely people's power. Under the leadership of the people's committee the Korean people set out on the building of democracy in their country.

But the Korean people's unanimous desire to develop their country into a unified independent and sovereign state has not been met.

The aggressive army of U.S. imperialism entered south Korea one month after the Soviet troops had routed the Japanese army. As soon as the aggressive army of U.S. imperialism came, the reactionaries began to raise their heads in south Korea. Soon the Korean people clearly realized that the U.S. imperialists did not want Korea's independence but were plotting to make Korea their colony.

It was already evident right after liberation that north Korea where the Soviet army had come and south Korea where the U.S. army had entered were moving in opposite directions.

In August 1945 the Soviet army issued its first declaration to the Korean people. It reads in part:

"Korean people! . . . Korea has become a country of freedom. However, this marks only the first page in Korean history. An abundant, fruitful orchard is the result of man's efforts and vigour. Therefore, the happiness of Korea, too, can only be achieved by the heroic efforts that you, the Korean people, will exert. Remember, Korean people! You have happiness in your own hands. You have attained liberty and liberation. Now everything is up to you. The Soviet army will provide the Korean people with all conditions for the free and creative labour you are bound to embark on. Koreans must make themselves the creators of their own happiness."

The Soviet army, as it had promised in this declaration, supported the people's committees in every way and provided all conditions for the Korean people to carry out democratic reforms and build a new happy life by their own hands.

In south Korea, however, the situation is totally different. The moment it arrived in south Korea, the U.S. army issued a proclamation in the name of MacArthur, which read in part:

"All powers of government over the territory fo Korea south of 38 degrees north latitude and the people thereof will be for the present exercised under my authority. Persons will obey my orders and orders issued under my authority. Acts of resistance to the occupying forces or any acts which may disturb public peace and safety will be punished severely.

"For all purposes during the military control, English will be the official language."

Carrying this proclamation into effect in south Korea, the U.S.

military government authorities dissolved the people's committees which had been established by the people themselves according to their own will and deprived our people of their rights to speech, press, assembly and association, and imprisoned and murdered patriotic people. The U.S. imperialists pursued the reactionary policy of turning the southern half of our country into their colony.

When the U.S.S.R.-U.S. Joint Commission met to carry out the decision of the Moscow three foreign ministers conference adopted in December 1945, the Soviet delegation made a determined effort for the establishment of a unified democratic government of Korea.

The U.S. imperialists, however, considered that if such a democratic united government should be established in Korea, their aggressive policy would be barred from being carried into reality. So, they stubbornly objected to the just Soviet proposal and torpedoed the decision of the Moscow conference.

The quisling Syngman Rhee and other reactionary elements in Korea are despicable traitors who betrayed the interests of the country and the people; acting upon the U.S. military government's directive, they came out against the decision of the Moscow conference from the beginning under the slogan of "anti-trusteeship." They helped the U.S. imperialists to frustrate the implementation of the decision of the Moscow conference which fully conformed to the Korean people's interests and to wreck the work of the U.S.S.R.-U.S. Joint Commission.

Thus, Korea, freed from the Japanese occupationers' oppression, has been artificially divided with the 38th parallel as the demarcation line, and the south Korean people find themselves again groaning under the rule of the foreign invaders, the U.S. imperialists.

2

The most vital task set before the north Korean people in building a unified and democratic independent state in the political situation prevailing in our country after liberation was to rally all the democratic and patriotic forces and create, in the northern half of our country, a solid political and economic base for the building of a united and democratic state.

In order to successfully carry out this task our Party set forth a fighting programme, which was:

1. To strengthen the people's committees, genuine people's government bodies, firmly relying on the Democratic National United Front which rallies all democratic parties, social organizations and patriotic forces;

2. To liquidate the evil aftermath of Japanese imperialist rule, the main obstacle to the building of a democratic state, grant democratic liberties—the freedom of speech, press, assembly, association and so forth, establish and strengthen the trade union and other democratic social organizations;

3. To abolish the feudal tenant system once and for all by enforcing an agrarian reform to confiscate the land owned by the Japanese imperialists and the landlords, and distribute it gratis to the landless or land-poor peasants. To nationalize factories, mills, transport services, banks, mines and forests of the Japanese imperialists and traitors to the nation, restore the factories and other enterprises, railways which had been destroyed by Japanese imperialism and improve the people's life;

4. To rear our own cadres for running the state, and introduce a democratic educational system and expand schools.

This fighting programme for the democratization of Korea conformed to the interests of all sections of the Korean people and had unreserved support and approval from them. Our Party unwaveringly led our people in their struggle to carry this programme into effect.

In 1946 a democratic election to the local people's committees was conducted and, on this basis, the North Korean People's Committee, the central organ of power, was established for the purpose of strengthening the people's committees—people's government bodies—and raising their role in the building of democracy.

The election to the people's committees was conducted on the principle of universal, equal and direct suffrage by secret ballot. The election was held under conditions in which the broadest masses of the people could freely express their true will. It was the first democratic election in the history of Korea.

At the election of the local people's committees 99.6 percent of the voters went to the polls. The number of those who were barred from taking part in the election according to the election rules was only 4,387 men, and they were pro-Japanese elements, insane persons or men who lost the voting right by court findings.

In this election 3,459 people were elected to provincial, city and county people's committees, of whom 510 were workers, 1,256—peasants, 1,056—office workers, 311—workers in the field of culture, 145—tradesmen, 73—entrepreneurs, 94—religious men and 14—from other fields.

Thus, the people's committees are genuinely people's organs of power composed of representatives of all strata of the Korean people on the basis of a strong allliance of the workers and peasants led by the working class. The people's committees were founded by the people themselves.

The elections to the local people's committees and the North Korean People's Committee legally consolidated the people's committees as organs of state power.

The people's committees rely on the broad masses in conducting their work, thoroughly defend the people's interests, faithfully serve the people, enjoy unqualified support of the entire people and maintain ties of kinship with them.

We had to carry out the democratic reforms without fail in order to assure the successful building of a democratic and independent state. Without the democratic reforms we would have been unable either to rehabilitate and develop the ruined national economy and radically improve the working people's life or to establish a people's democratic system in our country.

The first democratic reform was the agrarian refrom which was to emancipate the peasants, who made up some 80 per cent of the population, from the oppression and exploitation of the feudal landlords.

In March 1946 the Provisional People's Committee of North Korea announced the Agrarian Reform Law and confiscated 1,000,325 *chongbo* of land belonging to Japanese imperialists, traitors to the nation and landlords, which was distributed free to the peasants with little or no land.

As a result of the agrarian reform, the feudal land ownership, which was an obstacle to the advancement of our countryside, was liquidated, and the economic footholds of the landlords and local usurers, the prop of reaction in the countryside, were wiped out.

The agrarian reform emancipated the peasants once and for all from feudal exploitation and subjugation and made them the owners of land, thus materializing the centuries-old desire of our peasants, increasing their political enthusiasm, patriotism and zeal for production, and providing conditions for raising their material and cultural standards.

The agrarian reform opened up a new path for the development of our agriculture. The agrarian reform strengthened the ties between towns and the countryside and made it possible to solve smoothly the problem of supplying food to the people and raw materials to industry.

Following the agrarian reform, the nationalization of major industries, transport facilities, communications and banks formerly owned by the Japanese and traitors to the nation was carried out.

The Provisional People's Committee of North Korea promulgated the Law on the Nationalization of Industries on August 10, 1946. Under this law, the factories, mills, banks, transport and communications facilities, which had been owned by the Japanese imperialists, pro-Japanese elements and traitors to the nation, became the property of the state, of the entire people.

All these enterprises had come into being as a result of Japanese imperialists' cruel exploitation of the Korean people and their robbing of Korea. For nearly half a century the Korean people were compelled to work for the Japanese imperialists and their stooges, pro-Japanese elements and traitors to the nation, suffering from poverty and hunger.

As a result of the nationalization of industries, the production facilities which became the property of the people were used for the good of the working masses and constitute the basis for the rehabilitation and development of our national economy.

In north Korea, the nationalization of industries deprived the reactionaries and pro-Japanese elements of their economic footholds and made the state sector predominant in the national economy. As a result of the nationalization of industries, conditions for the planned development of the national economy were created. The workers now worked for themselves and for their country. A wide patriotic movement for increasing production unfolded among them which the history of our country had never known.

Along with the Law of Nationalization of Industries the Labor Law was promulgated.

During the occupation of Japanese imperialism the Korean workers were severely exploited and worked 12-14 hours a day. The conditions of women and juvenile workers were far more wretched. Labor protection and social insurance were nil.

The Labor Law announced by the Provisional People's Committee of North Korea brought about radical improvement in the working condition and material standards of workers and office employees.

According to the Labor Law the 8-hour working day was introduced for the factory and office workers and the 7-hour day for those who are engaged in harm-affected labor. The 5-6 hour working day was introduced for the children of 13-15 and child labor under 13 was forbidden. A paid leave of two weeks to one month a year is given to the factory and office workers, and all measures are taken for social insurance and labor protection.

As a result of the enforcement of the Law on the Equality of the Sexes, women who make up half of the Korean population, came to take part in the political, economic and cultural life of the state on an equal footing with men. Now 11,509 women are on the people's committees at all levels and 69 are deputies to the Supreme People's Assembly.

As you see, already in 1946 democratic reforms were carried out in all spheres of politics, economy and culture in the northern half of our country. We were confronted with the tasks of consolidating the great results of the historic democratic reforms, rehabilitating and developing the national economy in the shortest possible period of time and improving the material and cultural standards of the people. In the five years since liberation a huge amount of work has been done in our country so as to carry out these tasks.

There were many difficulties in rehabilitating and developing our industry. The Japanese imperialists destroyed industrial and transport facilities and flooded mines when they were defeated.

As a result of the colonial rule of Japanese imperialism, our people had no cadres of their own when the liberation came. We had neither competent technical personnel to rehabilitate and develop industry nor cadres to manage enterprises skillfully.

During Japanese imperialist rule the industry of Korea was subordinated to the Japanese economy as its appendage. Our industry which was marked by extreme colonial lopsidedness could not produce necessary machines, raw materials and other supplies on its own and its technical equipment was backward and outworn.

All the difficulties, however, were cleared up by the patriotic struggle of the entire Korean people. The Korean people courageously pulled through all these difficulties with great creative efforts and gained great successes in the struggle for the rehabilitation and development of the national economy.

We successfully accomplished the 1947 and 1948 plans for the rehabilitation and development of the national economy and embarked on the carrying out of the two-year national economic plan for 1949 and 1950. The two-year plan adopted at the second session of the Supreme People's Assembly set forth important tasks, which were:

1. To increase the rate of growth of production in order to exceed the prewar level of industrial production;

2. To liquidate the colonial one-sidedness of industry, a baneful aftermath of Japanese imperialist rule, and lay the foundations of an independent national economy;

3. To create material conditions to rehabilitate quickly, after the reunification of the country, the south Korean economy which was devastated by U.S. imperialism;

4. To raise the material and cultural standards of the people by increasing the production of major consumer goods.

The working masses in north Korea have risen as one man in the struggle for implementing the two-year national economic plan. At factories and other enterprises and on construction sites the workers are actively conducting emulation campaigns for increased production to fulfil the two-year plan before the set time.

More than 300,000 workers and technicians are participating in the emulation campaigns and many enterprises fulfilled their 1949 plans ahead of schedule.

In industry the target of 1949, the first year of the two-year plan, was topped by 2.8 percent and the 1950 plan is also being carried out successfully. At present, in response to the call of the workers of the Hungnam Chemical Factory and three other major enterprises in South Hamgyong Province, production emulation campaigns are afoot throughout north Korea to mark the fifth anniversary of the country's liberation. Many enterprises decided to implement their plans for the current year before August 15, and the Unryul Mine, the Hamhung Lorry Station and many other enterprises fulfilled their assignments under the two-year plan by the end of February.

In the past few years industry, the main sector of the national economy in north Korea, has made remarkable progress.

As compared with 1946 the industrial output grew by 53.3 percent in 1947, by 117.9 percent in 1948 and by 236.7 percent in 1949.

We have not only rehabilitated industry but also erected many new factories and mines and rebuilt and expanded them with modern techniques. In 1949 a glass factory was built in Nampo, the first of its kind in our country. This factory will supply various glass products to the building industry, and to inhabitants. The Kilju Paper Mill and the Pyongyang Electric Bulb Factory have been enlarged. The construction of the Munpyong Zinc Factory is successfully under way, and it will be one of the big enterprises in our nonferrous metallurgical industry. The Kangso Electrical Appliances Factory, which will start operation at the end of this year, will make a great contribution to the development of the national economy of our Republic.

New big hydroelectric power stations, metallurgical plants, machine-building factories and textile mills are under construction. The Pyongyang Textile Mill whose construction will be completed this year will produce four times as much fabric as was produced by the textile industry of north Korea during Japanese imperialist rule.

The production of some of our industries has already risen above the level of 1944, the record year during Japanese imperialist rule.

The production of machinery increased by 146.9 percent compared with 1944, and the production of light industry goods grew by 52.7 percent. The colonial lopsidedness of industry is eliminated by degrees and the foundation of the national economy is being laid. Industrial output is increasing from day to day, the internal accumulations of industries are rising, and all the weaknesses which remained in the industrial field are being rapidly eliminated.

But it must also be pointed out here that the artificial division of our country with the 38th parallel as the demarcation line is seriously interfering with the development of Korea's economy.

Today south Korea is not supplied with electric power, coal and various other kinds of goods which are produced largely in north Korea, and north Korea gets no supply of various industrial raw materials and farm produce from south Korea. In particular, the division of the country into north and south has greatly affected the economy of south Korea.

In the past five years we have also obtained great results in the rural economy. The agrarian reform boosted considerably the zeal for production of the peasants who became owners of land. Among the broad masses of the rural population a struggle for increasing the crop yields is forging ahead briskly and irrigation works are carried on as a movement of the people as a whole.

In the past the northern half was the industrial zone of our country and south Korea, its granary. However, owing to the aggressive policy of the U.S. imperialists a reactionary ruling system has been established in south Korea and the people of the northern half are unable to get food from the southern half. Under these conditions our people were confronted with an urgent task to convert the northern half of our country into a region fully capable of attaining self-sufficiency in food and raw materials.

Thanks to the correct policy of the Government of the Republic for the development of agriculture and the patriotic campaigns of the peasants for increasing production, we have solved the food problem in the main.

The volume of grain production in the northern half of the Republic exceeded by far the level of 1939, the year of the highest crop yield during Japanese imperialist rule. Compared with 1944, grain output grew by 10.4 percent in 1948 and by 9.8 percent even in 1949, a year hit by a severe drought. In 1949 cotton output increased by 91 percent compared with 1944.

Owing to the agrarian reform the material and cultural standards of the peasants rose markedly.

According to the investigations conducted by the Ministry of Agriculture and Forestry of the Democratic People's Republic of Korea in 1949 in 42 farm villages involving 2,466 peasant families, the number of primary schools in these villages was 7 times larger than that before liberation, clubs and libraries—48 times, primary school children—2.5 times, secondary school boys and girls—10 times and university students—6 times.

The grain output in these villages was 117,000 sacks in 1944 and 150,000 sacks in 1949. In 1944 the peasants in these rural areas had to borrow 8,000 sacks of food grain from the landlords because they were short of provisions after they paid their farm rent. In 1949, however, they paid 33,000 sacks of agricultural tax in kind to the state and kept all the rest of the grain harvests for their own use. Of this 10,000 sacks will remain in stock till next harvest even if they market 22,000 sacks.

The new houses which have been built in these villages in the past three years are 18 percent of all the farm houses there, and the number of the cattle bought in by the peasants is 628.

These facts, which are common occurrences in our rural areas, show clearly the extent of the progress of agriculture in the northern half of our country and of the improvement of the material and cultural standards of the peasants in the five years since liberation.

The state farms also play an important role in the development of our agriculture.

The northern half of our country has 15 state crop-growing and stockbreeding farms and nine breeding stock farms. They disseminate new farming methods and stock-raising techniques among the peasants and demonstrate the superiority of large-scale mechanized farming. They supply large amounts of improved seeds and breeding stocks to the rural villages.

According to the decision of the Government of the Republic, farm-machine hire stations were set up for the first time in the northern half in 1950, and they make it possible to improve the farming methods and introduce quickly the advanced agricultural techniques in the rural districts. Through the work of the farm-machine hire stations, our peasants are brought to realize the superiority of farm mechanization.

One of the tasks we are confronted with is to train our own cadres.

The future development and prosperity of our country depends wholly on whether or not we train competent cadres who are able to run the state and build the economy and culture, because the cadres decide everything and, moreover, we are very short of our own cadres.

Accordingly, we are directing major attention to public education and the building of culture and have gained great results in this field.

In 1949 primary schools in the northern half of the Republic were 2.8 times greater in number than in 1944 and their pupils 1.7 times. Junior and senior secondary schools increased 22 times and their students 23 times. The number of professional schools was up 12 times and their enrollment 10 times.

In the years of Japanese imperialist rule we did not have a single college. But today over 18,000 students are studying at 15 institutions of higher learning.

Besides, we are training tens of thousands of cadres through technical schools in factories and training centers for cadres on the job.

In the past we had no experience in rearing technical cadres on our own. But beginning this year we are sending to the work places engineers and assistant engineers we have trained for ourselves. In 1949, the graduates of specialized technical schools exceeded 3,500 and those of higher educational institutions were more than 1,100.

The campaign against illiteracy which was unfolded widely among the masses has now ended on the whole. At present over 2,300 elementary and middle schools for adults have been set up to give them systematic education, and about 160,000 working men and women are studying there.

Great success has also been achieved in the field of health services. Medical establishments have been set up in all parts of the northern half of the Republic; various infectious diseases which were evil aftermaths of Japanese imperialist rule have been wiped out and many holiday homes and sanatoria opened for the workers.

As you see, enormous is the success we have attained in the five years after liberation in the struggle for building a democratic independent state.

What has made our people gain such a brilliant success?

First, it is the establishment of the people's government in the northern half of the Republic and the fact that the democratic reforms carried out by this government are perfectly in accord with the interests of our people, and that these reforms guarantee a democratic development of our country; secondly, the Government of our Republic has the support of all the people who are united in the Democratic Front for the Reunification of the Fatherland, and the Workers' Party of Korea, which enjoys the support of the broadest masses of the people and is the most powerful political party in Korea, the guiding force for the Democratic Front for the Reunification of the Fatherland; thirdly, we correctly assimilated the rich experiences of the Soviet Union and the People's Democracies in our work.

All this guaranteed the victory of the people's democratic system in the northern half of our country.

The people in the northern half of our country are now advancing, with firm confidence, for the building of a united and democratic independent state.

3

The situation in the southern half of our country is diametrically different from that in the northern half.

The U.S. imperialists rejected the decision of the Moscow three foreign ministers conference on Korea and deliberately foiled the work of the U.S.S.R.-U.S. Joint Commission. They are converting south Korea into a military base for invading the East and a supplier of raw materials and a market for the monopoly capitalists of Wall Street.

Early in 1948 they turned down the just proposal put forward by the Government of the Soviet Union on simultaneously withdrawing the troops of the Soviet Union and the United States from Korea and leaving the solution of the Korean question to the Korean people themselves.

They unlawfully brought the Korean question to the UN General Assembly, fabricated the "UN Commission on Korea" by using their voting machine and, assisted by this commission, held a separate election in south Korea on May 10, 1948.

All the patriotic political parties, social organizations and people of Korea put up a stubborn struggle in opposition to the holding of a separate election in south Korea and the establishment of a separate puppet government.

A joint conference of representatives of political parties and social organizations of north and south Korea was held in April 1948 at the proposal of the Workers' Party. The conference was attended by representatives of 56 right, left and middle-of-the-road political parties and social organizations embracing over 10 million members. Only traitors like Syngman Rhee refused to participate in it.

The April north-south joint conference fully exposed the "UN Commission on Korea" as a tool for executing the U.S. imperialists' policy of colonial plunder. It decided on rejecting the separate election to be held in south Korea on May 10 and declared that the Korean people would not recognize a government, which would be established through this separate election, ruinous to the nation. Such a government could in no way represent the Korean people.

However, the south Korean reactionary clique and the U.S. imperialists held a separate election in south Korea by force of arms, terrorism and blackmailing and concocted a reactionary Syngman Rhee puppet government composed of traitors to the nation, the former lackeys of Japanese imperialism and the stooges of U.S. imperialism.

Among the so-called "members of the National Assembly" there is not a single representative of the workers or the peasants who are the overwhelming majority of the Korean people. This alone is enough to show the anti-popular nature of the reactionary puppet regime.

The establishment of a puppet regime through the separate election in south Korea is a trickery of the U.S. imperialists and their lackeys to perpetuate the artificial division of Korea. That is why the leaders of some 30 patriotic political parties and social organizations in north and south Korea held another conference in June 1948 and declared the separate election illegal and, at the same time, decided on holding a general election thoughout north and south Korea, founding a unified Democratic People's Republic of Korea and establishing a democratic central government.

The general election to the Supreme People's Assembly of Korea was held throughout north and south Korea on August 25, 1948. Although the pro-Japanese elements and traitors to the nation, relying on the arms of the U.S. imperialists, resorted to harsh repression and terrorism, 77.52 percent of the electors participated in the election in the southern half. In the north where the election wsa held in a free atmosphere, 99.97 percent of the electors went to the polls.

As you see, the Supreme People's Assembly is the supreme legislative body of Korea which has been established through an all-Korea election. The First Session of the Supreme People's Assembly proclaimed our country to be the Democratic People's Republic of Korea, adopted the Constitution and set up the Government of the D.P.R.K.

The Constitution of the D.P.R.K. confirmed by law the successes of all the democratic reforms carried out in the northern half of our country, granted true democratic rights to the working people and opened up broad vistas for founding a unified democratic state. The Constitution expresses the centuries-old desire of our people.

The Government of the Republic, which was approved at the First Session of the Supreme People's Assembly of Korea, was of a coalition cabinet, and it embraced representatives of major political parties and social organizations of north and south Korea. Thus, the Government of the D.P.R.K. which has been formed as a result of the general election is the only legal government in Korea and enjoys the support of the entire Korean people.

At the request of the First Session of the Supreme People's Assembly of Korea, the Soviet government has withdrawn its troops from our territory, recognized the D.P.R.K. and established diplomatic relations with our country.

The founding of the D.P.R.K. marked a new stage in the struggle of our people to build a unified independent country. All the patriotic political parties, social organizations and popular masses of Korea, firmly rallied around the Government of the People's Republic, are struggling with increasing stamina to consolidate the political and economic base of the Republic and promote national reunification.

The heroic people of south Korea are stepping up a powerful all-people struggle to overthrow the Syngman Rhee puppet regime which the U.S. imperialists and their stooges have rigged up against the will of the people.

4

North and south Korea are going different ways. As the days go by, the sharp contrast between the political and economic situations in north and south Korea shows more convincingly which is the right path leading the country and the people to prosperity.

The U.S. troops keep staying in south Korea even now when the Soviet troops have withdrawn from north Korea. The U.S. imperialists have concluded the "ROK-U.S. Agreement on

Military Assistance" and the "ROK-U.S. Agreement on Economic Assistance" with the anti-popular puppet regime and have converted the southern half of our country into their colony.

The southern half of our country ruled by the traitorous Syngman Rhee clique has been transformed into a land of darkness where reactionary terrorism and violent repression prevail.

Under the patronage of U.S. imperialists and their agent, the "UN Commission on Korea," the treacherous Syngman Rhee clique is harshly suppressing not only the left forces but also the right elements who are discontented with their reactionary rule. The Syngman Rhee police have arrested and imprisoned 12 "national assemblymen" in violation of the law which provides for their "inviolability."

Syngman Rhee murdered Kim Gu, a right-wing leader, simply because the latter had advocated the peaceful reunification of the country. The Syngman Rhee clique is slaughtering progressive men in the field of culture for not making statements in support of the puppet government.

Backed up by the bayonets of the U.S. imperialists, this clique is trying desperately to maintain its rule in south Korea by means of suppression, terrorism and massacre, and is even going to such length as destroying people en masse.

The appalling situation in south Korea brought about by the reactionary rule of the U.S. imperialists and the Syngman Rhee clique, their stooge, is calling forth the indignation and strong resistance of the working masses.

An extensive guerrilla struggle of the people is now under way throughout south Korea to oppose the colonial policy of the U.S. imperialists and overthrow Syngman Rhee's reactionary ruling system.

In this situation, an urgent need arose for all the patriotic political parties and social organizations of our country to take new measures to struggle for territorial integrity and national reunification.

With a view to rallying all the patriotic democratic forces in a more vigorous struggle against reaction, we organized the

Democratic Front for the Reunification of the Fatherland late in June 1949, which embraced 71 political parties and social organizations of north and south Korea.

The inaugural meeting of the Democratic Front for the Reunification of the Fatherland discussed the situation in our country and put forward a proposal for attaining peaceful reunification in order to liberate the people in the southern half who are groaning under the terrorist rule of the Syngman Rhee puppet regime, foil the scheme of the Syngman Rhee clique to launch a fratricidal war at the instigation of the U.S. imperialists, and save the country and the people.

The justness of this proposal is clear for all to see. In its proposal, the Democratic Front for the Reunification of the Fatherland demanded the immediate withdrawal of the U.S. troops from south Korea and the "UN Commission on Korea," a tool serving the aggressive ends of the U.S. imperialists, and the guaranteeing of lawfulness for the democratic political parties and social organizations and their freedom of activities. It demanded a general election throughout north and south Korea free from foreign interference, peaceful reunification of Korea, and the entire Korean people's choice of a state system of their own free will.

This proposal on peaceful reunification won enthusiastic support from the entire Korean people. But it did not agree in the least with the aggressive and anti-popular aims of the U.S. imperialists and the reactionaries, their lackeys, who were pursuing a colonial enslavement policy in south Korea. The Syngman Rhee clique could not accept this proposal because they were aware that they could maintain their rule only under the patronage of the U.S. armed forces. By turning down this proposal, they showed ever more clearly that they were afraid of the Korean people and betrayed their true colors as traitors to the Korean people.

The Korean people have risen in the struggle to overthrow the Syngman Rhee puppet regime that is obstructing the peaceful reunification of the country. This greatly alarms the U.S. imperialists. The U.S. imperialists have instigated the Syngman Rhee clique to launch frequent armed clashes along the 38th parallel in order to find a pretext to interfere in the internal affairs of Korea. At the same time, by using their voting machine, they have resorted to such underhand manoeuvres as to illegally place the Korean question again on the agenda of the fourth session of the UN General Assembly and dispatch the third "UN Commission on Korea."

The Korean people are well aware of the aims of the "UN Commission on Korea."

The first "UN Commission on Korea," a tool of the U.S. imperialists in carrying out their colonial enslavement policy in Korea, was sent to our country to legalize the separate election in south Korea and the establishment of the Syngman Rhee puppet regime. The mission of the second "UN Commission on Korea" was to justify the Syngman Rhee puppet regime terrorizing and massacring the people under the manipulation of the U.S. imperialists. And the third "UN Commission on Korea" is scheming to save the Syngman Rhee puppet regime from ruin and make Korea a permanent colony of U.S. imperialists.

Recently, with the start of the aggressive acts by the new "U.N. Commission on Korea," the traitorous Syngman Rhee clique is fussing about introducing a "UN police force" into south Korea under the manipulation of the U.S. imperialists and is even preparing for the formation of an alliance with the Japanese imperialists.

However, no aggressive intrigue of the U.S. imperialists will ever be realized. The Korean people do not want uninvited guests who are encroaching upon the independence and freedom of their country.

The U.S. imperialists must clearly see that the Korean people today are different from what they were yesterday.

Our people are not a flock of sheep who allow a pack of wolves to eat them up.

Today the Korean people have their fatherland, the Democratic People's Republic of Korea, and a powerful political and economic base. In the course of building democracy in the northern half of the Republic over the five years since liberation, our people have personally experienced true freedom and happiness as a people in power. The Korean people, who have been freed from 36 years of colonial oppression by Japanese imperialism, will not yield to anyone the rights and freedom they have won and will not become colonial slaves again. The Korean people will never allow the U.S. imperialists to subjugate and plunder their country.

Our people are now in a struggle to implement the proposal of the Democratic Front for the Reunification of the Fatherland on the country's peaceful reunification in order to attain complete national independence, develop the country along democratic lines and win peaceful reunification. A graphic illustration of this struggle can be seen in the fact that the people in the northern half of the Republic are energetically building democracy to strengthen the political and economic base of our Republic and that the people in the southern half are putting up a mass resistance and ever-growing guerrilla struggle against the U.S. imperialists and the Syngman Rhee traitorous clique, their lackeys.

The Korean people are by no means alone in their just struggle to win their country's complete freedom and independence. All the peoples of the world who love peace and democracy are supporting our struggle.

The Workers' Party, the Democratic Front for the Reunification of the Fatherland led by the Party, the Government of the D.P.R.K. and all the Korean people who are rallied around it, will advance vigorously for the complete independence and reunification of their country and for peace and democracy. They will certainly win the final victory.

Everything for the Postwar Rehabilitation and Development of the National Economy *(Excerpt)*

Report Delivered at the Sixth Plenary Meeting of the Central Committee of the Workers' Party of Korea, August 5, 1953

Comrades, the present Sixth Plenary Meeting of the Central Committee of our Party is convened under the new situation created in our country following the signing of the Armistice Agreement.

The heroic struggle waged by the Korean people for three years in defence of the country's freedom and independence against the U.S. imperialist armed invaders ended in victory for us. The U.S. imperialist aggressors suffered an ignominious defeat in their military adventure to turn our country into their colony and enslave the Korean people. The enemy was compelled to sign the Armistice Agreement because of his irretrievable military, political and moral defeat in the Korean war, and thanks to the tenacious and patient efforts of the Korean and Chinese peoples to restore peace in Korea, and to the public opinion and pressure of the peace-loving peoples of the world. Thus, the Korean people won a glorious victory in their Fatherland Liberation War.

In this sacred war our Workers' Party members fought courageously in the forefront of the entire Korean people.

Our Workers' Party played the role of the pivot and organizer in the Peoples' Army, and performed a great function in strengthening it. Members of the Workers' Party in the People's Army always bore the brunt of battles in any offensive or defensive, any mountain or field operation, courageously waging hand-to-hand fights. Our Party members constituted the backbone and acted as models in the People's Army.

Our Workers' Party members in the rear surmounted all hardships and difficulties in the face of barbarous enemy bombing under difficult wartime conditions; they restored and developed factories and mines, ensured railway transport, and steadily increased production in farming and fishing villages. Our Workers' Party members, in factories built underground, kept up munitions production for the front; assured the transport of war supplies to the front line satisfactorily by running trains and trucks even on dark nights and in defiance of the enemy's bombings; continued fishing in face of frenzied enemy warships; and ploughed and sowed with camouflaged oxen.

During the enemy's occupation, our Party members did not yield to the enemy at all, but fought and were victorious in guerilla warfare, holding high the banner of the Republic to the end. In the enemy's POW camps, too, despite all sorts of persecutions and barbarous massacre by the enemy, our Party members never gave in but defended to the last their honor as Workers' Party members, as well as the banner of our Republic.

Who but members of our Workers' Party could have ever organized so heroic a struggle at the front and in the rear? There is no doubt that if the members of the Workers' Party had not heroically fought at the head of all the popular masses, we would have failed to win, and would have been doomed to colonial slavery to the U.S. imperialists.

Today the Workers' Party of Korea, through its devoted, heroic struggle, has proved itself a reliable vanguard to which the Korean people can entrust their destiny and future without hesitation; it represents the wisdom and glory of the Korean people. Thus, our Party, in the struggle for safeguarding the country's freedom and independence and for a happier and more resplendent future of the people, has been strengthened and developed into a revolutionary party armed with all-conquering Marxist-Leninist theory. In the Fatherland Liberation War, our Party, as a member of the "shock force" of the international working-class movement, made a tremendous contribution to the consolidation of the camp of democracy and socialism and to the safeguarding of world peace.

I feel a boundless pride at the fact that I, as a member of so glorious a party as the Workers' Party of Korea, share this great honor with you.

On behalf of the Sixth Plenary Meeting of the Party Central Committee, I extend warm thanks to all the functionaries and Party members in the People's Army, factories, urban communities, farming and fishing villages, on the railways, in interior service organs, self-defence corps, garrison troops, Party and state organs, cultural institutions, and social organizations.

Also, in the name of the Sixth Plenary Meeting of the Party Central Committee, I express warm gratitude to the members of all the democratic political parties and people of all walks of life who, shoulder to shoulder with our Party members, fought actively for the freedom and independence of the country against the U.S. imperialist armed invaders.

And I extend warm gratitude and congratulations to the men and officers of the Chinese People's Volunteers who aided us in our struggle for the freedom and independence of our country at the cost of their blood.

I express warm gratitude to the peoples of the great Soviet Union, China and other People's Democracies, as well as to their Communist and Workers' Parties, for the continuous and unselfish aid they gave us during the period of peaceful construction and especially during the war.

I extend profound thanks to the people of good will all over the world for rendering active support and encouragement to the sacred cause of the Korean people.

1. On the Armistice and the Question of the Country's Reunification

Comrades, the armistice signifies a great victory for us. Though the armistice did not bring complete peace to Korea, the conclusion of the Armistice Agreement marked an initial step towards the peaceful settlement of the Korean issue, a first exemplary contribution to the relaxation of international tension. By concluding the Armistice Agreement, we have come to open up the possibilities for the peaceful settlement of the question of our country's reunification.

It is wrong to think, as some comrades do, that war might soon break out again and that peaceful construction could not be undertaken because the armistice does not mean a complete peace. It is likewise a wrong tendency to be indolent, lax and self-contented, thinking that an end has been put to war and complete peace is ensured in our country. The point is to consolidate the victory embodied in the armistice, which we have won at enormous sacrifices by going through the tribulations and calamities of war, and to struggle unremittingly for a lasting peace in Korea and the peaceful reunification of the country.

The first and foremost task confronting us in connection with the conclusion of the Armistice Agreement is to struggle persistently for a complete peaceful settlement of the question of our country at the forthcoming political conference. The basic aim of the political conference is to get all the troops of the United States and its satellite countries to withdraw from south Korea, and to enable the Korean people to settle the Korean issue by themselves, and to prevent foreigners from interfering in the internal affairs of our country. We have consistently advocated the peaceful settlement of the Korean issue—the peaceful reunification of the country. It is quite evident that if the U.S. imperialists had not interfered and if the Korean question had been solved in accordance with our line and claims, our country would have long ago been reunified, and our country and people would have been freed from all the sufferings and disasters resulting from the country's division. Our task is to carry our just line and claims into effect and to do everything for their realization.

The Korean nation is one and Korea belongs to the Koreans. The Korean question must naturally be settled by the Korean people themselves. The Korean people absolutely do not want to remain split. No aggressive force can break the desire and will of the Korean people for the reunification of their country.

The forthcoming political conference should naturally reflect and defend the just claims, desire, will and fundamental interests of the Korean people. Therefore, our people will under no circumstances tolerate, and thoroughly reject, any plan or plot of the imperialist interventionists contrary to them.

With the political conference approaching, the U.S. imperialists are already making a fuss behind the scenes. Notwithstanding the signing of the Armistice Agreement in which it was stipulated that the chief aim of the political conference is to discuss the question of withdrawal of foreign troops from Korea, the notorious warmonger Dulles, U.S. Secretary of State, concluded the so-called "ROK-U.S. Mutual Defence Pact" with the traitor Syngman Rhee. This pact is aimed at stationing aggressive forces of the United States in south Korea indefinitely and, whenever necessary, unleashing another criminal war of aggression in Korea, in violation of the Armistice Agreement. The "ROK-U.S. Mutual Defence Pact" is an aggressive pact which allows U.S. imperialism to obstruct the peaceful reunification of our country and interfere in our domestic affairs. It is a glaringly country-selling pact under which the Syngman Rhee clique sell the southern half of our country to the U.S. bandits. To conclude such a pact at a time when the political conference is in the offing is an act hindering a reasonable solution of the Korean question at the political conference. It can be easily foreseen that they will seek to throw the political conference into confusion, resorting to all sorts of intrigues, obstructive tactics and provocations at the conference, just as they did during the truce talks.

We, however, must by all means fulfil the just claims and demands of the Korean people by relying on the powerful support and encouragement of the peace-loving peoples all over the world, and by the unanimous will and struggle of the Korean people, just as we did in the course of the truce talks. Thus, the political conference should certainly be brought to the expected results and our country reunified peacefully without fail. To attain this goal, we must wage an unremitting struggle.

All our Party members and people should not relax their keyed-up attitude and, without slacking off in the least, should increase their revolutionary vigilance to a high degree, keep a close watch on every movement of the enemy, and be ready at all times to see through the enemy's vicious designs and frustrate them in advance.

All the Party members and the entire people should rally still more firmly around the Party Central Committee and the Government and do their utmost to increase the might of the country in every way. We have ample conditions and possibilities to carry out triumphantly this task which confronts our nation, our state and our Party.

Today, following the armistice, the situation in south Korea has been plunged into hopeless chaos. Antagonisms and contradictions are being further aggravated within the enemy camp, and the life of the people becomes more and more wretched. Growing and gaining in scope among the masses of the people are hatred and rebellious trends against the U.S. imperialist aggressors and the traitorous Syngman Rhee's reactionary rule which is maintained by their bayonets. The enemy's military, political and economic crises are becoming more grave. This will no doubt provide a favorable condition for the Korean people in their struggle for the peaceful reunification of the country.

The task is to arouse to the struggle for the peaceful reunification of the country all democratic, patriotic forces of the popular masses throughout the country, rallying them around our Party and Government, and to make it possible to settle the Korean question by Koreans themselves, by repudiating the colonial occupation policy of the U.S. imperialist aggressors and the traitorous rule of their lackeys, and by compelling the U.S. forces of aggression to withdraw.

Report of the Central Committee of the Workers' Party of Korea to the Third Congress (Excerpt)

April 23, 1956

For the Peaceful Reunification of the Country

Comrades, the disastrous results of the rule for ten years of the U.S. imperialists and the Syngman Rhee clique over south Korea are now glaring in all spheres of the life of the south Korean people.

All the goings-on in south Korea show that the reactionary Syngman Rhee government which represents the interests of a handful of comprador capitalists and landlords, is not only an anti-popular setup for the oppression and exploitation of the working masses but also an instrument of U.S. imperialism's Korean aggression, one which is at pains to usher in the influence of U.S. imperialism. The treacherous regime in south Korea is a faithful servant of the U.S. imperialists in carrying out the latter's new war and colonial enslavement policies.

The puppet Syngman Rhee government is openly calling for a prolonged stationing of the U.S. troops. It has left the south Korean economy entirely under the domination and control of the U.S. monopolies; it is frenziedly expanding the puppet army which is the U.S. imperialists' cannon fodder for aggressive war; and is strengthening the barbarous fascist ruling machine.

In south Korea today all the major levers of control over the economy and the state's economic life have been placed in the hands of the U.S. imperialists.

The whole world knows that the aim of the United States' so-called "economic aid" to other nations lies in establishing its military and political domination over them, and this is most glaringly and shamelessly in evidence in south Korea.

Most of the U.S. "aid" to south Korea has been spent on the armament of the puppet army and the building of military installations, and the remainder has been allocated to the purchase of U.S. surplus goods which find no outlet in the world market.

Through this "economic aid" the U.S. imperialists have gained absolute power over the operation of all the major production facilities and economic establishments in south Korea, and the "ROK-U.S. Combined Economic Board" which they set up to exercise this power, decides upon or controls all the industrial, financial and monetary policies of the puppet government.

Thus, the puppet government is barred from managing the economy of the state at its discretion, and is subject to the approval of the "Board" even to work out budgets and taxation plans.

The U.S. imperialists, exercising control over the south Korean economy, directly plunder strategic materials such as tungsten and copper produced in south Korea. They have paralysed its industry and subordinated it wholly to U.S. monopoly capital by making the major production establishments entirely dependent on the raw materials and supplies brought from the United States.

In consequence, the colonial lopsidedeness and distortion of the south Korean industry have further increased. Many small and middle manufacturers and tradesmen are going bankrupt and ruined owing to the floods of U.S. goods, the rise in the prices of raw materials and supplies imported from the United States and exorbitant tax burdens.

Even the cotton textile industry which was eking out a bare

existence in south Korea is forced to suspend operations indefinitely and going bankrupt owing to the forcible sale of cotton goods and hikes in cotton prices by the U.S. imperialists.

The U.S. imperialists' "economic aid" and enslavement policy towards south Korea ensure them maximum profits and enable them to easily realize their political and military aims to turn south Korea into their military base.

In order to hoodwink the peasant masses of south Korea who were influenced by the agrarian reform in north Korea, the Syngman Rhee clique has carried out an "agrarian reform" and is shouting noisily, "Landlords are no more and the conditions of the peasantry have improved."

However, the conditions of the peasantry are far from improved, and they are subjected to ever more cruel exploitation and oppression. Under various names such as "redemption grain for the price of land," "land acquisition tax," forcible grain purchase and farm rent, the peasants are robbed of the greater part of their annual harvests by the puppet government and the landlords. Consequently, the "distributed" land is falling back into the hands of the landlords and rich farmers, and more and more peasants are sliding down into the status of tenant farmer or farm hand with no land; or they are leaving the farms.

Moreover, the south Korean peasants are suffering from various exacting levies and usuries and falling into the bondage of debts to the landlords and rich farmers. Thus, the total liabilities of the peasants were 18,000 million *hwan* as of November 1954. This means that each peasant household in south Korea has a debt of 8,791 *hwan* on an average.

In spite of such an appalling economic situation in south Korea, the Syngman Rhee clique, faithfully carrying out instructions from the U.S. imperialists, is imposing stupendous burdens upon the people in order to reinforce the puppet army and rearrange and extend the military bases.

The degenerated American way of life prevails in the social life of the south Korean people and everything that is national is despised and humiliated; even trifling utterances and behaviors of "politicians" of the opposition parties are subject to ruthless suppression, not to speak of progressive ideas and views.

In south Korea the people are denied even elementary democratic liberties and rights, and it has turned into a prison of people where terrorism and massacre are rampant.

Subjected to two- or three-fold oppression and exploitation by imperialism, feudalism and comprador capital, the people's life in south Korea is sliding into a slough of unbearable poverty and absence of rights. This impels the south Korean people to rise in a struggle against U.S. imperialism and the Syngman Rhee clique for existence, freedom and national rights.

Today the struggle of the people in the southern half is not in high tide, but there is no doubt that inspired by all the achievements in the northern half, they will resolutely rise in a struggle for the democratic reunification of the country.

Such, in brief, is the situation in the southern half of the Republic.

The division of the country spells distress and misery not only for the people of south Korea under the oppression of the U.S. imperialists and the Syngman Rhee clique, but also for the entire Korean people, and it presents the main obstacle and threat to the social development of our country.

Before the Korean people there remains as ever the national task of achieving the country's democratic reunification and complete national independence by struggling against the U.S. imperialists' aggressive forces and their allies in the southern half—the landlords, comprador and pro-American elements—and by liberating the south Korean people from imperialist and feudal oppression and exploitation.

This means that our revolution is still in the stage of the anti-imperialist, anti-feudal, democratic revolution from the national point of view, and that it has a long, rugged and tortuous way to go.

In carrying out the anti-imperialist, anti-feudal, democratic revolution, we must further consolidate the people's democratic system in the northern half and, at the same time, unite the people in the southern half, especially all the patriotic, democratic forces aspiring to reunification and independence on a democratic basis.

The motive power of our revolution is the people in the

northern half who are united on the basis of the worker-peasant alliance led by the working class, and the working class, the peasantry—its most reliable ally—and the broad sections of the small propertied classes opposed to the U.S. imperialist and feudal forces in the southern half. Even the national capitalists who desire the country's reunification and independence on democratic lines can join in the anti-imperialist, anti-feudal struggle.

The struggle of the Korean people against U.S. imperialism is directly connected with the struggle of the peoples throughout the world for peace, democracy and socialism, and it is a major link in the struggle of the Asian peoples in defence of national freedom, independence, and stable peace against the aggressive policy of U.S. imperialism.

This international solidarity of the national-liberation struggle of the Korean people is a decisive factor hastening the complete victory of our revolution.

We must drive out the U.S. imperialists from Korea and struggle against the reactionary, traitorous regime of the Syngman Rhee clique for the peaceful reunification and independence of the country. To do so, we must firmly rely on the ever-growing strength of the democratic and socialist camp of the world and, on this basis, properly organize the mobilize the internal forces of our revolution and intensify the national unity and solidarity.

Comrades, the Party line with regard to the peaceful reunification of the country along democratic lines—the basic task of the Korean revolution at the present stage—is the only correct one in view of the situation prevailing at home and abroad. Our Party, therefore, has consistently held and will hold to the line of the peaceful reunification of the country.

After the armistice alone, we advanced many concrete proposals for the reunification of the country in statements or resolutions of the Democratic Front for the Reunification of the Fatherland, of political parties and social organizations, among them the proposal for north-south negotiations adopted at the Eighth Session of the Supreme People's Assembly.

However, the Syngman Rhee clique, a faithful stooge of U.S.

imperialism, catering to the will of their master, turned down all our proposals for national reunification. Moreover, they keep on with provocative acts along the Military Demarcation Line in flagrant violation of the Armistice Agreement, and they call for a prolonged stationing of the U.S. troops, openly clamoring about the so-called "march north expedition" to resume the fratricidal war.

They have largely expanded the fascist police machinery and are ruthlessly suppressing all the patriotic forces in the southern half. They are persecuting in every way all groups and persons not belonging to their own faction, to eliminate them from the political life of the state.

Even though the Syngman Rhee clique opposes our proposals for the peaceful reunification of the country and perpetrates all sorts of traitorous acts, this by no means precludes the possibility of peaceful reunification.

Hearing of our proposals for peaceful reunification, the workers, peasants, students, scientists, workers in the cultural field and all the conscientious patriots in the south, before anyone else, will not remain passive and allow the anti-popular, treacherous crimes of the Syngman Rhee clique.

Of late, the number of people yearning for the country's peaceful reunification keeps growing in the southern half. More and more personages are discontented with Syngman Rhee's rule and sympathize with the distressed people in the south. As Mr. Kim Gu and Mr. Kim Gyu Sik did in the past, they come forward in support of the idea of negotiations between north and south Korea. Thus, an ever-increasing aspiration is manifested in our country for another such historic meeting as the north-south joint conference of April 1948.

Our Party warmly welcomes and supports this patriotic aspiration, and is fully prepared to join hands with those people at any time.

In this situation, we must take concrete steps to isolate the U.S. imperialists and the Syngman Rhee clique still more in the southern half and further expand the patriotic forces which strive for peaceful reunification.

The greatest obstacle to the strengthening of our internal forces for the peaceful reunification and independence of the country lies in the fact that under the fascist dictatorship of the Syngman Rhee clique, the loyal servant of U.S. imperialism, the people in the southern half are denied even the elementary democratic liberties and rights. Therefore, a fighting slogan of the Party for the moment is to win the democratic rights for the people in the south.

In south Korea the freedoms of speech, press, assembly, association and religious belief must be restored to the masses, and the freedom of political activities ensured for all the patriotic political parties, social organizations and individual persons.

The right to elect and be elected must be granted equally to all people in south Korea, irrespective of their property status, education, religious belief or sex, so that the broad masses of the working people, among them the workers and peasants, in particular, have the opportunity of actively participating in the political life of the state. Thus, the workers and peasants who constitute the majority of the population must be reprsented in the National Assembly of south Korea, and the National Assembly must be conducted in conformity with the will of the broad sections of the people to represent the interests of all social section and strata.

Conditions must be created to struggle against U.S. imperialism and the Syngman Rhee dictatorship, to eliminate the corrupt rule in south Korea and fight for the peaceful reunification of the country. At the same time, the economic life of the south Korean people must be stabilized so as to induce their patriotic enthusiasm and activity in the struggle for peaceful reunification.

In order to rehabilitate and develop the ruined national economy of south Korea, assure an independent development of its national industry and stabilize the livelihood of its population, a resolute struggle must be waged against the infiltration of U.S. monopoly capital and the forced import of surplus goods from foreign countries.

A struggle must be launched to check the growth of unemployment and price hikes, to raise the real wages of the workers and office employees, and to introduce an eight-hour day and social insurance for them.

We must oppose the policy of expropriating the peasants from land and forcibly taking away their grain, their exploitation through murderous usury and all types of levies imposed on them. We must deliver the yearly increasing numbers of food-less peasant families and peasants giving up farming from their misery, and struggle to make the tiller the owner of the land.

In order to protect the small and middle manufacturers and tradesmen from the oppression of the U.S. imperialist monopoly capitalists and comprador capitalists, they should be accommodated with funds and guaranteed conditions for pro-curing raw materials and selling their products.

With the common aim of peacefully reunifying the country, we also advocate, and are fully prepared for, a coalition with all the political parties, social organizations and individual person-ages in south Korea.

With a view to achieving such a coalition and forming a united front comprising all the patriotic political parties, social organi-zations and all persons with national conscience, we hold that a joint conference of political parties and social organizations of north and south Korea be called. If conditions are not yet ripe enough to hold such a conference, we are ready to conduct negotiations with individual political parties, social organiza-tions and patriotic peronages.

Those who join this coalition, which aims to achieve the peaceful reunification of the country, will be absolved from whatever crimes they committed before, and they must be al-lowed to take part in the coalition government to be formed after the country's reunification according to their merits and talents. Their property and social positions will be safeguarded.

One of the most important questions in facilitating the peace-ful reunification of the country is to effect political, economic and cultural contacts, travel and correspondence between north and south Korea.

For the exchange of goods necessary to the livelihood of the people between the north and the south, we can supply electricity, coal and timber which the people of the southern half badly need. We will keep the doors open to all the delegations and individual personages who desire to come to the north for constructive and business-like purposes, guaranteeing them the freedom of activities and providing them with every facility in the northern half.

We propose that a permanent commission be set up which will discuss and take effective measures for all matters, ranging from the question of promoting contacts between the north and the south to that of reunifying the country. Representatives of the governments, the highest legislative organs, political parties and social organizations and independent personages will participate in this commission by an equal ratio between north and south Korea.

We think that under the prevailing situation, such measures are most practical and workable, provided both sides are sincere enough to meet the desire of the Korean people.

To put into effect all our proposals and points mentioned above, the armistice must be consolidated and converted into a lasting peace before anything else. We demand that while all the provisions of the Armistice Agreement are strictly observed, the armed forces of both sides be reduced to the minimum so as to lighten the people's burdens of military expenditure and divert the released funds to peaceful construction. Further, the separate military pact concluded between the "government" of south Korea and the United States Administration must be repealed.

For the Koreans to settle the Korean question for themselves, all foreign troops including the U.S. imperialist forces of aggression and the Chinese People's Volunteers should be withdrawn and there should be no foreign interference in the internal affairs of our country.

At the same time, the countries interested in the peaceful solution of the Korean question should convene an international conference with the participation of representatives of the north and south Korean governments, and create practical conditions for settling the Korean question in a peaceful way.

Comrades, the road ahead of our struggle for national reunification and independence along democratic lines is beset with innumerable difficulties and obstacles. However, this road alone can lead our contemporary generation to happiness and all our posterity to welfare and prosperity.

Therefore, if we keep to this line of struggle and stubbornly fight for its realization, we will have all the more ardent support from the entire Korean people and will enjoy the positive encouragement and support of the peace-loving forces of the world.

And our Party will become an invincible force and triumphantly carry out the glorious task of national reunification and independence on democratic lines.

Report at the Tenth Anniversary Celebration of the Founding of the Democratic People's Republic of Korea

(Excerpt)

September 8, 1958

Comrades, today, when we are celebrating the tenth anniversary of the founding of the Republic with great victories in socialist construction, the south Korean people are still suffering under the colonial oppression and exploitation of U.S. imperialism.

South Korea is now facing ruin in all spheres of its political, economic and cultural life.

The U.S. imperialists have completely seized the important arteries of the south Korean economy, and have geared them entirely to the realization of their policies of military aggression and colonial plunder.

The so-called "aid" given by the United States is an important tool of aggression in south Korea. In south Korea, the U.S. monopoly capitalists have gained control of all economic sectors, and they have utterly destroyed its national economy.

South Korean industry, which was backward to start with, has sharply declined, chained to U.S. monopoly capital. Over 90 percent of the few remaining factories and enterprises are medium and small enterprises with fewer than 50 workers. Today more than 80 percent of these medium and small enterprises have fully or partially suspended operations because of the shortage of raw materials, power and funds under the pressure of U.S. monopoly capital and a handful of comprador capitalists.

The mining industry of south Korea, said to have been in relatively good shape in the past, is also in a deplorable situation now.

Today south Korea's industrial output is only half the preliberation level and industry's contribution to the total national income of 1957 was no more than 8.6 percent. This indicates that the Syngman Rhee clique can squeeze nothing more out of south Korean industry.

With the total bankruptcy of south Korea's industry, the Syngman Rhee clique has used the rural areas as its main field of exploitation and plunder. But today even the rural areas are in a state of irretrievable bankruptcy.

The planted area in south Korea has dwindled by 600,000 *chongbo* and the gross output of grain by 40 percent compared with the time of Japanese imperialist rule. Thus, south Korea, which was formerly known as the granary of our country, has been reduced to an area of chronic famine which has to import more than 5 million *sok* of grain every year. In North and South Cholla Provinces, the rice-producing centers, more than 80 percent of total peasant households ran out of food last spring.

Although industry is being destroyed and rural areas are being devastated in this way, the Syngman Rhee clique, faithful henchman of the U.S. imperialists, is frenziedly increasing armaments by persistently bleeding the people white. The national economy is going bankrupt and the people's living conditions are deteriorating more and more, but the military expenses are on the steady increase every year.

In 1957, military expenses were 3.6 times those in 1953. The Syngman Rhee clique is intensifying its plunder of the working people in order to maintain the huge puppet army of more than 600,000 men as a tool serving the aggressive policy of the U.S.

imperialists. Today, the bulk of the budget of the south Korean puppet government is appropriated for military purposes. In 1957, military and police expenses in the budget of the puppet government amounted to around 70 percent.

The Syngman Rheeites, in order to meet their enormous military expenses, continuously increase all kinds of tax burdens upon the popular masses. In 1957, the tax revenue of the puppet government was 5.3 times that of 1953. The working masses, extremely impoverished because of uninterrupted cruel plunder, are now totally unable to bear the heavy tax burdens. According to the "results of the implementation of the financial programme" for the first half of this year, made public by the Ministry of Finance of the puppet government, actual revenue was no more than 34.3 percent of the estimated total amount. This means that their finances are totally bankrupt and that the working masses have been so impoverished that nothing more can be squeezed out of them by any terroristic or coercive means.

As its financial difficulties increase, the puppet government has no choice but to allot almost all the budgetary revenue to the upkeep of the army and police. The actual outlay in the first half of this year amounted to only 37.1 percent of the estimated expenditure, more than 96 percent of which was allocated for military and police and administrative expenses, and only 0.01 percent for agriculture.

The workers of south Korea are receiving starvation wages, barely one-third of the minimum living cost, and in quite a few cases they are not paid even those wages for over half a year. More than 90 percent of the peasants are shouldering enormous debts and many of them are abandoning their farmland to wander from place to place, unable to endure the robbery of the landlords and usurers. In south Korea today, the number of the unemployed and semi-unemployed has reached more than 4.2 million and hundreds of thousands of child beggars are wandering about the streets.

Today's south Korea, as even its rulers themselves admit, is undergoing its "greatest hardships in 4,000 years."

The American way of life and misanthropy are corrupting

ethics and morality in south Korea, and defiling the ancient national culture and the beautiful manners and customs of our people. Thus, darkness and degeneration prevail throughout south Korean society.

Such is precisely the outcome of 13 years of the U.S. army occupation and the sellout rule of Syngman Rhee after liberation.

Comrades, how can the south Korean people find a way out of this catastrophe? Only by forcing the U.S. imperialists, who are occupying south Korea, to withdraw from there and by reunifying the divided country as soon as possible.

The source of all the sufferings and miseries of the south Korean people today is the occupation of south Korea by the U.S. imperialists.

The Chinese People's Volunteers are now returning from Korea to their homeland. They have already completed their second-stage withdrawal and will complete their withdrawal from Korea by the end of this year.

However, the U.S. imperialists, far from taking their dirty talons off south Korea, are causing more tension and seriously jeopardizing peace in Korea by continuously expanding their armaments and are even bringing in guided missiles and atomic weapons.

But the enemy will never frighten the Korean people this way.

There is no excuse for the U.S. armed forces to remain in Korea any longer. They must immediately stop their reckless provocative acts and pull out of south Korea.

Everyone who is anxious about the fate of his fatherland and who wishes national prosperity should resolutely join in the struggle against the U.S. imperialist occupation of south Korea. All Koreans who have a national conscience, from workers and peasants to entrepreneurs and merchants, should join efforts and fight to force the withdrawal of U.S. troops.

Now is the time for all classes and strata in south Korea to draw a lesson from the national calamity and misery caused by 13 years of U.S. imperialist occupation of south Korea and the division of our country.

Representing the vital interests and aspirations of the entire

Korean people, our Republic has, from the first days of its foundation, waged a tireless struggle for peacefully reunifying the divided country. We put forward just and realistic proposals that we Koreans meet for negotiations and reunify the country by ourselves in a peaceful way without foreign interference.

However, the Syngman Rhee puppet clique, together with the U.S. imperialists, answered this proposal with an armed invasion against our Republic.

Following the armistice the Government of the Republic, with a view to converting the truce into a lasting peace and easing the tense situation, repeatedly proposed that both the north and the south reduce armaments, renounce the use of armed force against each other and guarantee free economic and cultural exchange.

However, even today, the puppet clique has answered these proposals with "march north" clamors. The traitorous Syngman Rhee clique has even refused to accept our offer to send relief supplies, precious fruits of the labor of the north Korean people, to the numerous unemployed people and orhpans of south Korea.

In an endeavour to prolong its last days, the Syngman Rhee clique does not hesitate to violate the national interests in every way.

Therefore, the first and foremost question to be solved for the peaceful reunification of the country is to change the war provocation and sellout policy of the Syngman Rhee puppet clique.

First of all, the basic democratic liberties and rights of the people should be ensured in the political life of south Korea.

Today south Korea is under an out-and-out fascist terrorist rule, and even those who merely utter the words "peaceful reunification" are punished by law.

All political parties and social organizations should be ensured the freedom of political activity and, especially, the workers and peasants who comprise the overwhelming majority of the population should be free to participate in all political institutions, including the "National Assembly."

To restore the utterly devastated national economy of south Korea and raise the extremely low living standards of the people, it is necessary to change the traitorous policy of the Syngman Rhee clique and effect economic exchange between the north and the south.

In the northern half of the Republic, the foundations of an independent economy have been laid and the powerful heavy and light industry bases have been built. Electricity, coal, steel, cement, chemical fertilizer and others abundant in the northern half are the precious assets for our people to build Korea into a rich and strong, independent and sovereign state. We ardently desire that all the valuable riches we have created will be used to rehabilitate south Korea's economy and free its people from penury.

The Government of the Republic has, on a number of occasions, offered to supply south Korea with electricity, coal, cement, chemical fertilizer, etc., through economic exchange between the north and the south.

All these proposals have not materialized because of the rejection on the part of the Syngman Rhee puppets.

We can no longer tolerate the traitorous policy of the Syngman Rhee clique which is opposing the unanimous desire of the Korean people for their fellow countrymen to visit each other freely and live in harmony and unity. All the south Korean people should actively participate in the struggle for opening up economic exchange between north and south Korea. This is one of the important steps for relieving the south Korean people from bankruptcy, and hastening the peaceful reunification of the country.

It is of great importance to form in south Korea a united front of all patriotic, democratic forces opposed to the U.S. imperialists and the traitorous Syngman Rhee clique in order to hasten the peaceful reunification of our country. Today, in south Korea, the interests of not only the workers and peasants but all strata including intellectuals, youth and students, handicraftsmen and national capitalists, with the exception of the tiny handful of Syngman Rhee puppet clique, are in sharp conflict with the aggressive policy of the U.S. imperialists. This means that possibilities have further matured for the formation of a united front of the patriotic forces in south Korea.

All people desirous of changing the present catastrophic situation of south Korea must unite as one. All people who demand the withdrawal of U.S. troops and who oppose the treacherous policy of the traitorous Syngman Rheeites must join the united front.

We positively support the growth of the patriotic, progressive forces in south Korea. We will support and fight together with all the political parties, social organizations and public figures who fight for the improvement of the living standard of the south Korean people, for their political freedoms and rights, and stand for the peaceful reunification of the country. We will fight together with anybody who opposes the U.S. imperialists and the traitorous Syngman Rhee clique and who wants to work for the peaceful reunification of the country, without asking about his past.

The struggle of the Korean people for the peaceful reunification of the country is an arduous one.

However, when the socialist forces in the northern half develop still more and all the patriotic, democratic forces in south Korea unite and rise in the national-salvation struggle against the U.S. imperialists and traitorous Syngman Rhee clique, the peaceful reunification of the country will certainly be achieved.

Comrades, we cannot but be concerned about the recent situation of our compatriots in Japan.

The Kishi government is intensifying its persecution of our compatriots in Japan. The Kishi government is not only refusing to recognize their legal rights but is even committing the inhumane act of using our compatriots held illegally in Japanese detention camps, as bait for bargaining with the Syngman Rhee clique.

Our compatriots in Japan, who are deprived of all their rights and suffer national discrimination and difficulties in daily life, recently expressed their desire to return to the Democratic People's Republic of Korea.

Our people warmly welcome the desire of our compatriots who, having lost their livelihood in Japan, want to come back to the bosom of their homeland.

Our fellow countrymen in Japan, as citizens of the Democratic

People's Republic of Korea, which is prospering and developing with every passing day, have a legitimate right to return to their country and lead a happy life together with their compatriots at home.

The Government of the Republic will provide our compatriots in Japan with all facilities for leading a new life after their return to the homeland. We regard this as our national duty.

Speech at the 15th Anniversary Celebration of the August 15 Liberation, The National Holiday of the Korean People (*Excerpt*)

August 14, 1960

Comrades, the building of socialism and the happy life of the people in the northern half of the Republic are exerting a tremendous revolutionary influence on the people in south Korea and immensely encouraging and inspiring them in their struggle against the U.S. imperialists and their lackeys.

The aggressive policy of the U.S. imperialists and the reactionary rule of the Syngman Rhee clique have reduced south Korea to a complete colony of the United States and a military base for launching another war. Fifteen years' occupation of south Korea by the U.S. imperialists since liberation has ruined south Korea's economy and driven its people into the mire of hunger and poverty.

The broad masses of the people in south Korea could no longer tolerate all the social evils and the appalling difficulty of living that results from U.S. colonial rule, and at last they rose in the heroic resistance struggle against the oppressors.

The mass uprising of the people which broke out throughout

57

south Korea this spring was the explosion of the long pent-up grievances and resentment of south Korean people against U.S. imperialism and the Syngman Rhee clique. It was a just struggle demanding freedom and liberation, a new government and a new life.

In defiance of the armed suppression by the enemy, the broad sections of the people, including the youth, students and intellectuals, in south Korea fought heroically and overthrew the Syngman Rhee puppet government. This is the initial, great victory gained by the south Korean people in their struggle against the U.S. imperialists and their lackeys. Through their valiant struggle, they demonstrated the revolutionary mettle of the Korean people and, at the same time, gained precious experience and lessons.

The uprising of the south Korean people has shown that no amount of threat of the bayonet or deceptive tricks can enslave the people long or check their revolutionary struggle. The uprising has also shown that when the people are united and rise in the struggle against the oppressors, they can smash any stronghold of the imperialists, and that they can triumph only by mass struggle.

However, the recent struggle of the south Korean people was not carried on to the last, to a complete victory. This was because the broad masses of workers and peasants failed to take part in the struggle. Thus, the south Korean people have not yet won liberty and democracy, and their demands have not yet been realized.

For the south Korean people to win complete victory of democracy the broad masses of workers, peasants and other people should join in the struggle, which must be thoroughly anti-imperialist and anti-feudal.

So long as an aggressive army of foreign imperialism exists in his territory, no one can speak of his national independence nor can the people live in peace. At present, the root cause of our country's division and of all misery and sufferings of the south Korean people lies in the occupation of south Korea by the aggressor army of the U.S. imperialists and their aggressive policy. As long as south Korea is in the grip of that army, the peaceful reunification of our country will never be realized, nor will the south Korean people be free from the present miserable plight.

The U.S. imperialist aggressor army which is occupying south Korea is the ringleader of the reactionary forces there. It is a band of robbers plundering the south Korean people of their properties and perpetrating all sorts of atrocities. This imperialist aggressor army of the United States, the ringleader of reaction and gansterism, is the primary target in the struggle of the south Korean people.

Therefore, the workers, peasants and all other sections of the population in south Korea must, first of all, resolutely oppose the U.S. imperialist aggressive forces and fight to force their army out of south Korea. When all the patriotic people in south Korea rise as one in the anti-U.S. struggle, these aggressors will be unable to stay there but will be compelled to withdraw.

The anti-imperialist struggle of the south Korean people must be linked with the anti-feudal struggle. In implementing their aggressive policy, the U.S. imperialists use and actively protect feudal landlords, comprador capitalists and reactionary bureaucrats in south Korea. The feudal landlords and comprador capitalists on their part serve to extend the influence of the aggressive forces of U.S. imperialism in south Korea and, in collusion with them, are oppressing and exploiting the people. Without fighting the feudal forces, therefore, the anti-imperialist struggle cannot be waged successfully, nor can the anti-feudal struggle be successful without fighting the aggressive imperialist forces.

Only when all the patriotic forces—the workers, peasants, youth, students, intellectuals, entrepreneurs, traders, etc.—are united as one man and launch a decisive struggle against the aggressive forces of U.S. imperialism and the feudal forces, can the south Korean people attain real freedom and liberation and win complete victory of democracy.

For the development of all patriotic and democratic movements in south Korea, full democracy should be ensured, above all, in political life. In a society where the people's free will is overridden and fascist oppression and terror are rampant, only corruption and degeneration will prevail and there can be no progress at all.

In south Korea today, the questions of the country's peaceful reunification and north-south negotiations are a topic of discussion.

However, certain reactionary circles in south Korea are scheming to resume suppression against the trend. The reactionary attempt to restore the same rule of fascist terror as that of Syngman Rhee clique and destroy even the rudimentary gains made by the people at the cost of their precious blood must be smashed.

The south Korean people still have no elementary democratic rights and liberties. There is no freedom of speech, press, association, assembly or religion, and all progressive ideas and patriotic movements are suppressed. Especially communist ideology is still under a ruthless suppression.

If it is free to believe in Jesus Christ, why should it not be free to choose communist ideology?

Communist ideology is the most scientific and most progressive of all ideologies. One thousand million people in the world have already won freedom and liberation under the banner of communism and are enjoying a happy life. Communist ideology is gripping the hearts of increasing numbers of people on the globe; it is a banner of liberation and victory for them. In the northern half of the Republic communist ideology has become the dominant one, and the people have built a new, free and happy life under the banner of this ideology. Why, then should it be banned and suppressed in south Korea?

Historical experience has proved that communist ideology is winning one victory after another and those who suppress it are bound to perish.

Needless to say, it is free for any individual to accept communist ideology or reject it. No one does or can force it upon others. But no ideas should ever be suppressed.

Everyone should be guaranteed the right and liberty to choose whatever ideology he likes, to express his views, and to propagate his ideals.

Moreover, freedom of association and assembly and a complete freedom of activities of every political party and social organization should be ensured. In south Korea at present there is no political party which represents the workers and peasants who comprise the vast majority of the population. Neither the Liberal Party nor the Democratic Party in south Korea is a workers' or peasants' party and neither of them can represent the interests of the working people. Workers and peasants must have their own political party which can represent their will and can fight for their interests. Such a political party must also have a legal status.

In north Korea, since right after liberation, the Democratic Party, a political party of the propertied classes, has been enjoying a legal status and freedom of activity. Why should the political party of the laboring people be banned in south Korea? It is another question which class has its political party in power, but the workers and peasants should also be able legally to organize a political party of their own, and this party too should have complete freedom of activity. Denying this is nothing but ignoring the will of the broadest masses of the working people and stifling their interests.

Only when freedom of expression is provided to every class and section of the population, particularly to the broad masses of the workers and peasants, and only when a complete freedom of activity is guaranteed to all political parties and social organizations including the party of the working people, will south Korean society be able to make progress and its people successfully carry out their struggle for national and social emancipation.

Today the U.S. imperialists, dismayed at the awakening of the south Korean people and their unceasing struggle, are resorting to every trick to maintain their colonial rule over south Korea. They are bringing new-type weapons into south Korea, reinforcing their troops there and intensifying war preparations, while frantically trying to put the paralysed puppet ruling apparatus in order. The south Korean reactionary clique is trying to dampen the fighting spirit of the people by means of repression and deception, faithfully carrying out the orders of their American masters.

The recent "elections to the National Assembly" held in south Korea are a glaring manifestation of such machinations of the U.S. imperialists and their stooges. The south Korean ruling circles are very noisy about the "elections," describing them as "most fair." In fact, however, these "elections" were also a fraud, effected with money, deception and terror, like all the previous "elections" held in south Korea. Everywhere south Korean people destroyed polling stations and ballot boxes, assaulted police stations and other puppet government organs, declared the elections null and void and held demonstrations. Through these mass struggles they laid bare the true nature of the so-called fair elections. The present "National Assembly," too, like that under Syngman Rhee's rule, has not a single representative of the workers and peasants.

Needless to say, such a "National Assembly" cannot be a representative organ of the people.

The south Korean rulers are prating as if the "new National Assembly" and the "new government" could practise democracy, rehabilitate the economy and stabilize the people's living. But this is no more than a trick to deceive the people.

South Korea has now been ruined irreparably in all fields of politics, economy and culture.

The U.S. imperialists' policy of ruthless colonial plunder and militarization has totally devastated the economy of south Korea.

South Korea has turned into a market for U.S. goods, and its industries are being ruined under the pressure of U.S. monopoly capital and the handful of comprador capital. The number of factories has been reduced to half compared with that in the years of Japanese imperialist rule, and most of the remaining medium and small enterprises have stopped or curtailed operation because of raw material shortage, lack of funds and markets, and heavy tax burdens. Agriculture, which holds an overwhelming proportion in south Korea's economy, has been extremely devastated. As compared with the closing years of Japanese imperialist rule, the sown area has been reduced by 600,000 *chongbo* and the grain output decreased by more than 6 million *sok*. Every year south Korea suffers from an acute food crisis, and it has become an area of chronic famine.

Today the south Korean people are in an indescribably wretched plight. The wages of the workers are less than one-third of the minimum living costs, and even their payment is usually overdue a few months, sometimes more than half a year. Peasants are cruelly exploited by landlords and usurers. Most of them are under heavy debts, and over one million peasant households run out of food every year. Millions of unemployed and semi-employed are on the verge of starvation, and hundreds of thousands of children are wandering around and begging in the streets.

How can the south Korean rulers cope with this situation and meet the demands of the people? How can they rehabilitate the bankrupt national industry and rural economy, give jobs to the millions of unemployed, and save the broad masses of the people from hunger and poverty?

So long as the U.S. imperialists keep occupying south Korea and our country remains divided, no one, however he may come into power, can save the ruinous situation in south Korea and meet the demands of the people. Nothing will change and, if anything, the Syngman Rhee government would be renamed, say as Syngman Chang government. But their status and fate would be the same. Nor would there be any improvement in the people's life. This has been fully proved by the experience of the past 15 years since liberation.

The south Korean people demand liberty and the right to live and, above all, the solution of the burning problems of living. Unless these fundamental problems are settled, the struggle of the people will go on and gain in scope and strength.

No amount of repression and trickery by the U.S. imperialists and their stooges can put out the flames of the struggle now raging in south Korea, or keep them from growing fiercer.

On the occasion of the 15th anniversary of the August 15 Liberation, I, on behalf of the Workers' Party of Korea and the Government of the Republic, extend militant greetings to the south Korean people who are heroically fighting against the

U.S. imperialists and their lackeys, and convey to them the warm support and encouragement from the people in the northern half.

Comrades, the only way to save the present situation in south Korea and finally solve the Korean question lies in driving out the U.S. army and reunifying the country peacefully.

The peaceful reunification of our country must be achieved independently by holding free general elections throughout north and south Korea on a democratic basis without any foreign interference. This is our consistent stand on the question of national reunification.

The proposal of our Party and the Government of the Republic on the question of peaceful national reunification reflects the unanimous desire and interests of the entire Korean people and, accordingly, enjoys their unreserved support and approval. The bankruptcy of Syngman Rhee's clamors for "march north," and the ever-growing demand of the people for peaceful reunification in south Korea, conclusively testify to the correctness and vitality of our proposal for reunification.

The south Korean rulers are now compelled by the pressure of the people to speak of peaceful reunification. But they are only paying lip service to it; in reality they keep obstructing it.

Claiming that the "elections should be held only in north Korea," or that the "elections should be held under the UN supervision," they refuse to hold free, democratic elections.

Because Syngman Rhee wanted to maintain his one-man despotism at the expense of national interests, he was afraid of free north-south elections more than anything else. But why should one be afraid of the free elections if one truly stands for national independence and the interests of the people?

Why can't we Koreans solve the Korean question by ourselves? Why should foreigners meddle in this matter? This is an unbearable insult to our nation and it is designed to keep our people forever in the bondage of foreign imperialism.

The Korean people have a long history of thousands of years and time-honored cultural traditions. Today they have built a fine, new society by their own hands on half their territory and turned out as one for a complete liberation and prosperity of their country; they are a nation courageous, hardworking, resourceful, patriotic and strong in their sense of unity. Our people are capable of independently and admirably deciding their destinies without any others' interference.

The south Korean rulers say that they cannot accept a free north-south general election because it means "collaboration with the Communists" and involves the danger of being "communized."

However, those who really want to fight for the people and defend the interests of the nation will never be afraid of the Communists or oppose "collaboration with the Communists," because the Communists always work for the people; they are the most ardent defender of the national interests and the staunchest patriots. This was why the Japanese imperialists feared the Korean Communists more than anybody else and repressed them most ruthlessly.

Who was it but the Korean Communists that courageously fought against the Japanese imperialists, with fidelity to the revolution and the nation to the last moment, undaunted in the enemy's prisons or on the gallows? Who was it but the Korean Communists that, undergoing indescribable tribulations in the darkest period of Japanese imperialist rule, put up the 15-year-long bloody struggle with arms in their hands solely for the freedom and independence of the country?

Following liberation, the people in the northern half, under the leadership of the Communists, have firmly seized their destinies in their hands, upheld the independence and honor of their country and built a new, happy life. If communism was something bad, how in the north could the national economy develop so rapidly, towns and villages be built so beautifully as never before, the people's living standards improve daily and the national culture blossom so splendidly?

In the north there are a million members of the Workers' Party, the people have long accepted communist ideology; they are closely united under its banner.

In Korea national reunification precluding the Communists is even inconceivable. To do so means negating stern reality and, in effect, is tantamount to perpetuating the division of the country.

We Communists always maintain that we will closely unite and co-operate with all the political parties, social organizations and individual personages that fight for peaceful reunification and national independence. We will co-operate with all persons, regardless of their past, if they come out for the peaceful reunification of the country.

Only the stooges of foreign imperialism who betray the interests of the nation will be afraid of Communists.

No political parties, social organizations or individual personages can oppose "collaboration with the Communists" or reject free north-south elections if they are really concerned about the destiny of the nation and desire peaceful reunification.

There is no denying the fact that the most reasonable and realistic way to peaceful national reunification is to hold free north-south general elections on a democratic basis without any foreign interference. We appeal to all the political parties and social organizations and the people of all walks of life in south Korea to come out for holding such elections.

If the south Korean authorities still cannot agree to free north-south general elections for fear of the whole of south Korea being communized, then, we must work out, to start with, even transitional measures for settling the burning problems of the nation.

As one of such measures, we propose that a Confederation of north and south Korea be instituted. We propose to establish the Confederation by way of setting up a supreme national committee composed of the representatives of the Government of the Democratic People's Republic of Korea and the Government of the "Republic of Korea" mainly to regulate the economic and cultural development of north and south Korea in a uniform manner, while retaining, for the time being, the present political systems in north and south Korea and maintaining the independent activities of the two governments.

The establishment of such a Confederation will enable the north and the south to understand and co-operate with each other by ensuring contacts and negotiations between them and remove mutual distrust. We consider that, if the free north-south general elections are held under such circumstances, the complete peaceful reunification of our country can be realized.

In particular, the establishment of such a Confederation will make it possible to save south Korea from economic ruin by having the supreme national committee consider economic and cultural matters beneficial to the whole nation and ensure economic and cultural exchanges and mutual co-operation between north and south Korea, even though the Confederation does not mean the formation of a united coalition government representing all social strata and therefore cannot exercise united state leadership.

It is the most urgent question at present to put the national economy in south Korea on the right track and improve the people's living which has been extremely deteriorated.

As we have consistently held and realities prove, this question cannot be solved unless the economic interchange between the north and the south is put into effect.

It is a rudiment of political economy that no country can develop light industry and agriculture or improve the people's living standards without heavy industry.

In our country such a heavy industry exists in the northern half. After liberation the working people in the north have, by their devoted labor, built powerful bases of heavy industry and laid the foundation of an independent national economy. We have also a large number of our own technical cadres and rich experience in economic construction.

We earnestly hope that the electricity, coal, steel, cement, timber, chemical fertilizer and various machines and equipment which are turned out in quantities in the north will be used for the rehabilitation of the economy and the improvement of the living conditions of the people in south Korea. We eagerly desire to share with our brothers and sisters in south Korea all the results and experience we have gained in developing the economy, science and technology.

Only by relying on the powerful economic foundation of the northern half can south Korea overcome the shortage of raw and other materials and funds, and develop its industry by putting the bankrupt industrial establishments into normal operation and building more factories. In the rural areas agricultural production can be quickly increased by carrying out large-scale irrigation projects and through an ample supply of fertilizer and farm machines. Without rehabilitating south Korea's industry and agriculture in this way it will be impossible to provide the millions of unemployed with jobs or to solve the pressing problem of the people's living.

It is only empty phrase-mongering to talk about saving south Korea from economic ruin without economic exchange and co-operation with the northern half.

Certain persons in south Korea blare that foreign capital should be introduced for the development of its economy and even advocate inviting Japanese capital which had long controlled the economy of our country. Through their bitter experience they had under Japanese imperialist rule, and through the realities of south Korea today, the Korean people know too well what the inroad of foreign capital means. Why must we invite foreign capital instead of turning to account the sufficient economic means that exist in our own country? Such insistence is tantamount only to attempting to push south Korea's economy further into an irreparable bankruptcy, an economy which has already been seriously devastated because of its subordination to U.S. monopoly capital.

If we exploit the rich resources of our country and develop our national economy in a uniform way, with the united strength of our 30 million people and on the basis of heavy industry in the north, we will all be able to live as well as others.

Anyone who is concerned about the wretched plight of the millions of unemployed and child beggars in south Korea and has the slightest concern about the future destinies of our ragged, hunger-stricken compatriots there, will not oppose the economic exchanges and economic co-operation between the north and the south.

If the south Korean authorities consider that even the Confederation we propose is still unacceptable to them, we once again propose that a purely economic commission composed of representatives of the business circles of north and south Korea be set up to exchange goods between the north and the south and to co-operate with and help each other in economic construction. Thus, we must, first of all, relieve the brothers and sisters in south Korea from hunger and poverty, setting aside the political question.

Along with the economic exchange between the north and the south, cultural interchange should be conducted on an extensive scale and the people allowed to travel freely.

The Korean nation is a homogeneous nation with the same language, spoken and written, and has inherited the same historical and cultural traditions. However, we have been separated from each other for fifteen years, unable to visit each other, meet each other and even write to each other. Consequently, even our language is gradually changing in a different way in the two zones, and so are our culture and customs. Worse still, decadent Yankee culture and American way of life hold sway and our national culture and the beautiful customs of our people are being trampled upon in south Korea.

This hinders the uniform development of our nation and, in particular, threatens the danger of plunging south Korea into an inescapable quagmire of corruption and degeneration.

We should under no circumstances allow ourselves to ruin the future destiny of the nation on account of political antagonism and thus commit crimes indelible for generations to come.

We once again propose that the mutual visit of cultural missions and mutual exchanges in science, culture, arts, sports and in all other fields be effected between the north and the south. At least, correspondence should be made possible between parents and children, brothers and sisters, relatives and friends, and the people allowed to travel freely across the country.

One of the important questions in improving the relations between the north and the south and particularly in normalizing the economic life in south Korea is the reduction of the armed forces. Today the maintenance of the huge army in south Korea is the greatest burden to the people.

We still hold that the U.S. army should be withdrawn from south Korea and the armies of north and south Korea be cut down to 100,000 or less respectively. This will constitute an important measure for easing tension in Korea and promoting peaceful reunification and, in particular, lighten the heavy burdens of military expenditure imposed upon the south Korean people. In our country an army 200,000 strong will be enough to discharge the duty of national defence.

All the above questions are burning issues awaiting urgent solution for the benefit of the Korean people and, above all, for delivering the South Korean people who are in dire straits. The current situation in south Korea does not brook even a moment's delay.

In order to solve these questions, representatives of north and south Korea should, first of all, get together and negotiate. Unscrupulously saying this is wrong, this is impossible, or something in a similar vein, even before meeting and talking with each other, is not a proper attitude favoring the solution of questions. Such an attitude benefits only the U.S. imperialists who are trying to keep our nation split and pit our people against each other and turn south Korea into their permanent colony. If we keep ourselves divided and our doors shut to each other, the situation will be further aggravated and south Korean people will suffer greater misery and hardships.

We propose to the south Korean authorities, political parties, social organizations and individual personages that representatives of north and south Korea meet at the earliest date in Pyongyang, Seoul or at Panmunjom to negotiate about all the above issues.

There is no reason why the Koreans, one and the same nation, should not meet together and negotiate. Why should we, people in the north, continue to hold talks with the Yankees about the question of our own country at Panmunjom, a place in our own land? Why should the south Korean people be deprived of their seats by the Yankees? The Yankees must pull out and Koreans should sit together and discuss the Korean question.

All political parties, social organizations and individual personages in south Korea should demand that the north and the south hold negotiations as soon as possible. All patriotic people in south Korea must struggle for economic and cultural exchange between the north and the south, for the reduction of the vast army of south Korea and for free north-south general elections.

The peaceful reunification of our country can by no means be easily achieved. We must not forget even a moment that the U.S. imperialists, the ringleader of world reaction, are occupying south Korea. The peaceful reunification of the country can be achieved only by a persistent struggle of all the Korean people.

When the socialist forces are further strengthened in the northern half of the Republic and all the patriotic forces in south Korea firmly unite and turn out in the decisive struggle against the U.S. imperialists and their lackeys, we will be able to drive the U.S. imperialist aggressors out of south Korea and accomplish the great historic task of the peaceful reunification of our country.

Report on the Work of the Central Committee to the Fourth Congress of the Worker's Party of Korea *(Excerpt)*

September 11, 1961

For the Peaceful Reunification of the Country.

Comrades, during the period under review the situation in south Korea has changed tremendously. The great achievements in socialist construction in north Korea have decisively moved the balance of forces between revolution and counterrevolution in Korea in favor of the revolutionary forces.

The main trend of south Korean developments today is that while the revolutionary forces striving for the peaceful reunification of the country and for democracy grow continually stronger, the counterrevolutionary forces, isolated from the masses of the people, resort to the adventurist means of military terrorism in a last-ditch effort to find a way out of their blind alley.

In the spring of last year the south Korean people, no longer able to endure corruption and tyranny under U.S. imperialist colonial rule, finally rose up in a heroic resistance struggle for a new government and a new life, and they overthrew the Syngman Rhee regime. This was a great victory for the south

Koreans in their struggle to save the nation. It was a telling blow to the U.S. imperialist policy of aggression in Korea.

The April Popular Uprising marked a new turning point in the south Korean people's anti-U.S. struggle for national salvation. During this resistance the political consciousness of the south Korean people increased remarkably. With the momentum of their resistance, the spearhead of the struggle gradually began turning against U.S. imperialism.

The popular uprising and subsequent developments in south Korea show that the U.S. imperialists can never subdue the south Korean people, no matter how bloody the repression they resort to.

At the end of the Chang Myon regime the political and economic crises became extremely acute in south Korea. Life for the people became unbearable. Corruption and social disorder deteriorated conditions with each passing day.

The broad masses of the people came to realize all the more sharply that without the peaceful reunification of the country they could not free themselves from poverty, complete lack of rights, and colonial slavery. A mass struggle demanding north-south exchanges, the independent, peaceful reunification of the country, and north-south negotiation, developed with great force. South Korean youth and students came out with a proposal for north-south negotiation and exchanges, and the vast masses of the people rose in response. The general trend rapidly turned in favor of the masses of the people who supported the peaceful reunification of the country.

Driven into a tight corner, the U.S. imperialists and the south Korean reactionaries embarked upon the adventurist path of setting up a fascist military dictatorship to try to maintain their precarious rule.

The establishment of the dictatorial military regime in south Korea testifies to the fact that the U.S. imperialists' position in Korea is weakened, not strengthened. This is nothing more than the death-bed frenzy of the doomed. No matter what they do, the U.S. imperialists can never save the irretrievable, disintegrating colonial system in south Korea. The fascist military rule rather inflames the struggle of the people and will hasten the ultimate collapse of U.S. imperialist colonial rule over south Korea.

South Korea today has turned into a land of darkness where all democratic freedoms and rights have been denied—into a slaughter house of the people rampant with mass terrorism and murder. The south Korean military regime has disbanded all political parties and social organizations, closed down all the progressive organs of the press, and has already arrested, imprisoned, or massacred more than 100,000 patriots and innocent people.

Political chaos and unrest are steadily growing in south Korea and the contradictions and conflicts within the military circles are sharpening to an astonishing degree. The south Korean economy is going from bad to worse, and mass starvation is sweeping the whole of the south. It can never be otherwise as long as U.S. imperialism dominates south Korea.

The military rulers of south Korea are now clamoring about "reform," "building a self-reliant economy," and "relief for the people." But these are nothing but deceptions designed to placate the people's discontent and intensify fascist suppression. Developments in south Korea are vividly revealing that such slogans are nothing but empty promises.

In south Korea power is completely held by the U.S. imperialists. Until the colonial rule of U.S. imperialism is abolished, the south Korean regime, no matter who may seize power, will inevitably represent the interests of the U.S. imperialists and their collaborators—the landlords and the comprador capitalists—and the position of the south Korean people cannot expect to improve.

By means of "aid," the U.S. imperialists have seized the main arteries of south Korea's economy, subordinated them to their military purposes and completely blocked the road to independent development of the national economy in south Korea. Reduced to a military appendage of U.S. imperialism, the south Korean economy is faced with unavoidable ruin.

South Korea's industry is bankrupt. Oppressed by American monopoly capital and comprador capital, national industry is disintegrating even more and is steadily advancing towards bankruptcy and ruin. The overwhelming majority of the national capitalists' enterprises consist of medium- and small-sized units and at present, more than 80 percent of these are either not functioning or are operating below capacity.

Today, south Korea's meager light industry is almost entirely dependent on American machinery, equipment and raw material.

The bulk consists of war industry which provides supplementary war materials on the spot to the American mercenaries. The masters of this war industry are the comprador capitalists under U.S. protection.

South Korean markets are overflowing with U.S. commodities from overseas, and imports from U.S. "aid" account for 80 percent of south Korea's total volume of imports, which is 20 times the total volume of exports.

Thus, south Korea today remains a backward agrarian region without an independent industry.

Alongside the bankruptcy of industry, the south Korean rural economy has also been utterly devastated.

Feudal landlordism still prevails in the countryside. The bulk of the "distributed land" for the peasants has again been massed in the hands of landlords and rich farmers, and the peasants are subjected to ruthless feudal exploitation.

The pillage and exploitation by the U.S. imperialists and the landlords have not only held back the development of south Korea's agriculture but have sapped it to the limit. Compared with pre-liberation years, cultivated land has gone down 200,000 *chongbo* and the area sown, 400,000 *chongbo*. U.S. imperialist aggressive troops have requisitioned more than 100,000 *chongbo* of land from the south Korean peasants for military use. With industry bankrupt and the rural economy completely disintegrated, agricultural technology is horribly backward.

The destruction and stagnation of agricultural productive forces have caused a sharp decline in production. Grain output in 1960 dropped to two-thirds of the 1937 pre-liberation level.

Economic bankruptcy and cruel exploitation by the landlords and comprador capitalists have reduced the working people to a state of indescribable misery.

More than 6 million working people, that is, half of the labor force of south Korea, are chronically unemployed or semi-unemployed.

The regime in south Korea annually appropriates more than 70 percent of its budget for military expenditure. To cover this, it is raising taxes even more. Soaring inflation caused by oversized military expenditure weighs heavily on the working people. As of July 1961, the volume of currency in circulation had increased 206 times and commodity prices 126 times in comparison with 1949. The tax burden of the south Korean people rose more than 10 times in the seven years after the war. The workers are forced to work 10-18 hours a day, while their wages are less than one-third of what they need to meet minimum costs of living.

The broad masses of peasants have been reduced to debt slaves of landlords and usurers. The amount of peasants' debts soared 20-fold in the postwar period. Each year tens of thousands of peasant families are ruined and are forced to desist from farming. Since industry cannot absorb the ruined rural population, most of them are wandering beggars.

Such is the outcome of 16 years' rule by the U.S. imperialists and their stooges. Such is the result of U.S. "aid" to south Korea.

The U.S. army's occupation of south Korea and their policy of aggression are the main obstacles to the peaceful reunification of our country and the democratic development of south Korean society. They are the root of all the present misfortunes and sufferings of the south Korean people. The U.S. imperialists have converted south Korea into their colony and military base; they are constantly menacing peace in Korea and are doing all they can to obstruct our country's peaceful reunification. They have utterly ruined the south Korean economy, plunged the people of the south into the depths of famine and poverty, and turned the whole of south Korea into a living hell of terrorism and tyranny. Countless patriotic people and innocent country-men are shedding their blood because of the atrocities of the U.S. robbers, and our sisters are insulted and walked over in south Korea.

Today the U.S. imperialists are stepping up their war preparations under the pretext of "protecting" south Korea from "communist aggression," and they are viciously scheming to drive the south Korean people into a fratricidal conflict.

U.S. imperialism is the principal target of the struggle of the people in south Korea and the sworn enemy of all the Korean people. As long as U.S. armed forces occupy the south, we cannot expect a durable peace in Korea and the peaceful reunification of the country, and the south Korean people cannot win genuine freedom and libearation.

In maintaining their colonial rule in south Korea, the U.S. imperialists rely on the landlords, comprador capitalists and reactionary bureaucrats who serve them as guides and faithful allies in their aggression. The landlord class, under U.S. imperialist protection, ruthlessly exploits and suppresses the peasant masses. The comprador capitalists make fortunes by bringing in American commodities and capital, by plundering our country's natural resources and selling them to their masters, and by supplying the American mercenary troops with war materials.

Thus, the revolution in south Korea is a national-liberation revolution against imperialism, and is, at the same time, a democratic revolution against the feudal forces. The basic demand of this revolution is to drive the aggressive forces of U.S. imperialism out of Korea, shatter its colonial rule, and achieve both democratic development in south Korean society and the reunification of the country.

Comrades, to carry on the anti-imperialist, anti-feudal struggle successfully and to emerge victorious, the south Korean people must have a revolutionary party which takes Marxism-Leninism as its guideline and represents the interests of the workers, peasants and other broad sections of the popular masses. Without such a political party, it is impossible to set forth a clear-cut fighting programme for the people, to solidly unite the revolutionary masses, and to carry on the popular struggle in an organized way.

Since there was no revolutionary party and no clear-cut programme of struggle and since, as a result, the workers and peasants, the main masses, failed to take part extensively in the resistance, the April Popular Uprising could not be carried through in an organized way; and the south Korean people were inevitably robbed by new puppets of U.S. imperialism of the gains they had paid for with their blood. In addition, leadership by a revolutionary party was lacking, and the masses of workers, peasants and soldiers were not awakened. Therefore, the south Korean people failed to prevent the seizure of power by fascist elements in the upper strata of the army and to organize an effective counterattack against the enemy's onslaught on democratic rights.

The people in south Korea must learn from this bitter experience. They must have an independent workers' and peasants' party—a party deeply rooted in the broad masses—and they must win legal status for it.

This political party, to be organized by the working people in south Korea, will have to unite all patriotic forces and fight for the realization of a thoroughly anti-imperialist, anti-feudal programme, and for the satisfaction of the urgent demands of the south Korean people.

The primary task before the south Korean people is to fight against the occupation of south Korea by the U.S. imperialists and to struggle for the withdrawal of the U.S. forces of aggression.

The south Korean people must thoroughly expose and smash the sinister design of the U.S. imperialists to pit our brothers against each other under the pretext of checking "communist aggression." The Korean people want no fratricidal conflict. There may be different ideas and different political points of view among us, but the differences should not be an obstacle to the country's peaceful reunification, much less a cause of war. The phrase "communist aggression" is a lie invented by the U.S. imperialists and is nothing but a smoke screen to justify their occupation of south Korea, cover up their intention to invade all Korea, and to hoodwink the people in the south. The south Korean people must rise up in an all-people resistance to frustrate U.S. imperialist policies of aggression and war preparations. Young people must fight against forced conscription. Workers must organize slowdowns and strikes to obstruct the enemy production of armaments and transport of war supplies. And the entire people in south Korea must fight against the construction of military bases and installations.

The south Korean people must resolutely condemn and curb the bandit actions of the U.S. troops—the contempt, plunder and slaughter of our fellow countrymen—and bridle the aggressors so that they cannot operate arbitrarily. They must unconditionally refuse to collaborate in any way with the U.S. army of aggression and should not give them even a single grain of rice or a single drop of water. The aggressors must be made to tremble before the resistance of the enraged people, and not a single foot of our land should be left for these aggressors to stand on. Thus, the U.S. troops of aggression should be forced to withdraw as soon as possible, all the shackling military and economic pacts concluded between south Korea and the United States repudiated, and the U.S. colonial fetters shaken off once and for all.

When all the patriotic forces in south Korea are firmly united as one and rise up resolutely in the anti-U.S. struggle, the U.S. imperialists will find it impossible to hang on in our territory. And they will be driven out of south Korea without fail.

At the same time the south Korean people must struggle against exploitation and oppression by the landlords and comprador capitalists who are in league with the U.S. imperialists. They must also fight for the democratic development of south Korean society.

At present there is an urgent demand in south Korea to democratize social and political life, carry out democratic reforms in economic and cultural areas, and resolve the problem of the people's living conditions.

The south Korean military regime has completely deprived the people of even the most elementary democratic rights, binding them hand and foot.

South Korean military rulers are intensifying their fascist suppression of the people, arresting and jailing large numbers of patriots at random on the pretext of combating communism. They have gone so far as to perpetrate the intolerable outrage of sentencing reporters to death merely because they stood for withdrawal of the U.S. imperialists and for reunification without outside interference.

The people in south Korea must smash the fascist dictatorship and fight for their democratic freedom and rights. Freedom of speech, press, association, assembly, demonstrations and strikes must be guaranteed and freedom of activities for all political parties and social organizations must be restored. The barbarous terrorism of the military regime must be stopped immediately. All patriotic political prisoners and innocent people under arrest or in prison must be released immediately, and both agents of U.S. imperialism and traitors to the nation must be punished.

Solution of the land problem is one of the most important tasks confronting the democratic revolution in south Korea. Unless this problem is settled and agricultural productive forces are freed from their feudal fetters, the peasant masses, who make up more than 70 percent of the population in south Korea, can neither be saved from hunger and poverty, nor stabilize their living conditions.

The south Korean peasantry must unite in one body and struggle to enforce a democratic agrarian reform and to put an end to the system of feudal exploitation. Land should and must be owned by the peasants who till it. The landlords' land must be confiscated and distributed without payment among the landless and land-poor peasants so that they can realize their age-old desire for land. Those who have opposed U.S. imperialism and contributed to the cause of the country's peaceful reunification may be compensated for their land.

Land requisitioned by the U.S. occupation forces for military use must be immediately restored to the peasants.

A thoroughgoing democratic agrarian reform must be enforced; at the same time land must be extensively reclaimed and divided for free among land-poor peasants and unemployed people who had been forced to abandon farming.

Exploitation of the peasants through various kinds of usury must be prohibited; their land debts, as well as all the debts of the poor peasants, must also be cancelled.

The liquidation of feudal relations in the south Korean countryside will not only pave the way for the development of the agricultural productive forces and ensure the improvement of the peasants' living conditions but will also create favorable conditions for the development of national industry.

Without an independent national industry neither the people's well-being can be prompted nor national independence achieved. The factories, mines, railway facilities and banks owned by U.S. imperialists, comprador capitalists and traitors to the nation should be confiscated and nationalized to smash the economic bases of foreign imperialism and the traitorous domestic forces and to develop national industry. In particular, middle and small entrepreneurs must be allowed to develop freely by protecting their sector of the economy and ensuring them raw materials, funds and markets.

The south Korean workers must struggle for the enforcement of an eight-hour day, social security, a wage increase and the improvement of working conditions. Jobs must be given to the millions of unemployed as soon as possible and the workers' wages raised to meet, at the very least, the minimum cost of living. Commodity prices must also be stabilized, and the tax burden of the working people drastically alleviated together with the abolition of miscellaneous charges.

There is no work even for the small number of scientists and technicians in south Korea, much less conditions and freedom for their scientific research. The minds of the people are poisoned by reactionary, decadent American culture, while the culture peculiar to our nation is trampled upon and left to rot. Scientists and people working in culture and art must fight the penetration of reactionary American culture, struggle to improve their living conditions, and bravely strive to build a democratic national culture which serves the nation's independent development and the people's interests.

South Korean student youth and intellectuals should fight against the militarization and commercialization of schools and for a democratic reform of the educational system. Universal, compulsory primary education must be enforced to educate all children of school age at state expense, and an extensive adult education system should be introduced to give the working people an opportunity to learn and to eliminate illiteracy.

In south Korea today various epidemics and chronic diseases are rampant owing to the people's wretched living conditions and the rulers' criminal indifference to public health. Countless numbers of sick people, denied medical treatment, are suffering and dying. A system of free medical service must be instituted to protect the health of the people, and state measures must be taken to eliminate different kinds of epidemics.

To democratize all aspects of life for people in south Korea, one of the major tasks is to ensure to the women of the south social status and rights equal to those of men. Women should be liberated from the humiliation of being mistreated and despised, their personal dignity should be respected, and they should be guaranteed an equal opportunity for education. They should be actively incorporated into the work of society, and they should be included under the principle, equal pay for equal work.

The U.S. imperialists are keeping 700,000 mercenary soldiers in south Korea. Command of the "ROK army" is in the hands of the U.S. imperialists: its commanders are American generals. The overwhelming majority of the south Korean army are peasants and workers in uniform. They are young working people pressganged into the "ROK army" by the minions of U.S. imperialism.

Men in the south Korean army are forced to level their guns at their fellow countrymen in north Korea and to fire upon their parents and brothers who fight for freedom and survival.

In north Korea there is no enemy of the "ROK army." The People's Army, an army of workers and peasants, never wants to fight its brothers in south Korea. The real enemies of the "ROK army" are the U.S. imperialists, who occupy our territory, and their flunkeys.

The south Korean army should no longer remain a blind tool of the U.S. imperialists in their suppression of the people's patriotic and democratic movements and their invasion of the whole of Korea. Rather, it should become a national army, a people's army, defending the interests of the workers, peasants and the rest of the broad popular masses against the foreign imperialists. Command of the "ROK army" should be wrested from the hands of the U.S. imperialists. The anti-popular military service system should be abolished. And the fascist military system should be turned into a democratic one.

The rank and file and the junior officers of the "ROK army" must not be deceived by the pernicious plot of the U.S. imperialists to make Koreans fight Koreans. They must come over to the side of the people, resolutely reject the orders of the American commanders and the traitorous clique in the upper crust of the "ROK army," and fight against the U.S. imperialists and their minions.

People can win freedom and liberation only through their own struggle. The south Korean people have a glorious tradition of heroic struggle against foreign imperialist aggressive forces and against domestic exploiters. The liberation struggles of the popular masses, such as the Kabo Peasant War, the March First Movement, the June 10th Independence Movement and the Kwangju Student Incident, have been waged without stop, and telling blows have been struck at the oppressors. When the vast majority of the popular masses rise up in a body to struggle against their oppressors, any imperialist stronghold can be smashed. The U.S. imperialists bragged that the Syngman Rhee regime was the strongest anti-communist regime in Asia. But it was overthrown precisely by the mass struggle of the south Korean people.

Workers, peasants, youth and students, intellectuals and the broad masses of the people in south Korea must valiantly rise up in the struggle against U.S. imperialism and its stooges for democracy and for the right to exist.

Comrades, the only way for the south Korean people to completely free themselves from their present tragic situation is to drive out the U.S. army, overthrow the fascist dictatorship and reunify the country peacefully. During their history of tribulations since the liberation sixteen years ago, the south Korean people have come to realize keenly that they cannot go on living with the country divided into north and south.

The only way to rehabilitate and develop the economy and

improve the people's living conditions in south Korea is to achieve the country's reunification by the united strength of north and south Korea.

Peaceful reunification of our country is the unanimous desire of all Koreans and the supreme national task which must be solved without delay.

The position of our Party on the question of Korean reunification is clear. The Party has consistently maintained that the question of reunifying our country should be solved independently by peaceful means based on democratic principles. The Korean people can and must themselves achieve peaceful national reunification.

To fully solve the question of our country's reunification, a unified government should be established by free elections on democratic principles throughout the whole of Korea without any interference from the outside forces. Separate elections in south Korea alone can never alter the situation. A unified government truly representing the people's will can be formed only through all-Korea elections in which the people in the northern half, and the workers, peasants and various other strata of the people in south Korea participate; and only by forming such a government can the south Korean people gain their freedom and rights and change the conditions in which they live.

We consider that such elections should be held on the principle of universal, equal and direct suffrage by secret ballot.

The reunification of Korea is an internal affair of our nation which must be decided by the Korean people of their own free will. There can be no expression of the people's free will as long as the country is occupied by the imperialist aggressive forces and outside interference is tolerated. The prerequisite for genuine free elections is to force the U.S. imperialist army of aggression out of Korea and to reject any interference from outside.

At the same time, freedom of political activities should be guaranteed throughout north and south Korea. All political parties, social organizations and individual public figures in both parts should be able to openly announce their political platforms, express their political views before the people without any restriction, and engage in free activity wherever they are in the country. Only when these conditions are ensured can the Korean people establish a unified government through genuine free elections.

The proposals of our Party and the Government of the Republic on the peaceful reunification of the country are most reasonable, realistic and fair. Our reunification programme enjoys the ardent support of the entire Korean people and the approval of the peace-loving peoples of all countries of the world. Only the U.S. imperialists and their followers, the traitorous reactionary forces, prevent the holding of free, general elections throughout north and south Korea and stand opposed to the peaceful reunification of the country.

Frustrating the obstructive manoeuvres of the enemy, all patriotic people in south Korea should courageously struggle for general elections throughout north and south Korea. Workers, peasants and other sectors of the people in the south should wage a stubborn fight for the withdrawal of the U.S. army of aggression and for the attainment of the independent, democratic and peaceful reunification of the country.

Although the Korean people's struggle for the peaceful reunification of the country is complicated by difficult twists and turns, the revolutionary situation is developing in our favor. All Koreans are eagerly awaiting the great event of national reunification, and the day of its realization is drawing nearer.

To fulfil this national aspiration the Korean people in the north and south should unite all their forces and enter the struggle against the U.S. imperialists' occupation of south Korea and for the country's peaceful reunification.

The most crucial necessity in the development of the revolution today is to form an anti-U.S., national-salvation united front in south Korea, embracing all patriotic forces. The workers, peasants, urban petty bourgeoisie, youth and students, intellectuals and even the national capitalists in south Korea are all suffering from the partition of the country and U.S. imperialist colonial rule. They are all linked by common national interests. The forces of all these classes and strata should be solidly united and directed in struggle against U.S. imperialism, the principal enemy of the Korean people. Only by doing so, can the south Korean people repel the common enemy, win the struggle for liberation and realize the cause of national reunification.

It is of utmost importance in forming an anti-U.S., national-salvation united front to strengthen the worker-peasant alliance under the leadership of the working class. The worker-peasant alliance should become the political and social basis of the united front.

While consolidating the worker-peasant alliance, efforts should be made to strengthen solidarity with the youth and students and intellectuals. They should be more extensively drawn into the anti-U.S., national-salvation struggle and should be made to go deeply among the broad masses of the people, including workers and peasants, and keep close ties with the popular masses.

Thus, the U.S. imperialists and their lackeys should be thoroughly isolated, all the patriotic, democratic strata in south Korea should be rallied under the banner of independent, peaceful reunification, and unity should be achieved between the patriotic, democratic forces of south Korea and the patriotic, socialist forces of north Korea.

We shall march hand in hand with those who struggle against U.S. imperialism without asking about their past, their class background, social status, political views and religious beliefs. We will warmly welcome even those who in the past committed crimes against the homeland and the people provided they repent their crimes and openly support the country's peaceful reunification. And we will not fail to embrace them at all times after the reunification.

We are now living in the age of the disintegration of the imperialist colonial system, in the great era of national-liberation revolution. Hundreds of millions of people who only yesterday were oppressed and exploited by foreign aggressors have won their freedom and independence, throwing off the colonial yoke. All the peoples of the world who groan under imperialist oppression are launching valiant struggles against the aggressors. The liquidation of colonialism is a trend of the times which no force can hold back.

How can our nation, with its long history and time-honored culture, put up with U.S. imperialist colonial rule and tolerate national humiliation and persecution in this great age of national-liberation revolution?

All those who love their country and people should unite and rise up in the save-the-nation struggle to expel the aggressors and reunify the country peacefully.

Once the entire Korean people firmly unite to combat the U.S. imperialist aggressors and their lackeys, they will be able to defeat the enemy, no matter how desperate he may be, winning a glorious victory.

The U.S. imperialists will be driven out of Korea and the cause of national reunification will unquestionably be achieved by the united might of the whole nation.

On the Immediate Tasks of the Government of the Democratic People's Republic of Korea *(Excerpt)*

Speech Delivered at the First Session of the
Third Supreme People's Assembly, October 23, 1962

Comrade Deputies, the great successes achieved in the construction of socialism in the northern half of the Republic are exerting a great revolutionary influence on the people in south Korea who are under the colonial rule of U.S. imperialism. These successes are moving the balance of forces between revolution and counterrevolution in Korea more and more in favor of the former.

Inspired by the great victories achieved by their north Korean brothers in socialist construction, the south Korean people rose up in a heroic struggle and overthrew the Syngman Rhee regime that had ridden roughshod over them for 12 years, and now they maintain a determined struggle against U.S. imperialist colonial rule and the military dictatorship.

Developments in south Korea since the April Popular Uprising show that no "legal" replacement of the regime nor establishment of a terrorist dictatorship by sheer force enables the U.S. imperialists to tide over the political and economic crises in south Korea or suppress the people's struggle there for democratic freedom, the right to live and the peaceful reunification of the country.

Despite bloody repression by the U.S. imperialists and the south Korean military regime, anti-U.S. sentiments are mounting among the broad masses of the people in south Korea, and the patriotic and democratic forces are gradually growing stronger.

In the year and a half following the seizure of power by the military fascist clique, the political and economic crises in south Korea have deepened. The economy has declined further, the people's living standards are deteriorating, and corruption and social disorder is increasing.

In south Korea all the political parties and social organizations have been dissolved, and martial law has been in force for more than a year now.

While launching an unprecedented barbarous attack on the democratic freedom of the people, the south Korean military regime is trying hard to quell the people's discontent, making a lot of talk about the "construction of a selfdreliant economy," a "five-year plan for economic development," or "relief for the impoverished." But no one expects that the south Korean military regime, a mere tool of U.S. imperialist colonial rule, will ever do any of these things. It has already become quite evident that all this is nothing but absolute nonsense.

The economy of south Korea under U.S. imperialist occupation is in a state of irretrievable ruin.

Having seized the key branches of the economy of south Korea, the U.S. imperialists have reduced it to their military appendage and have totally destroyed the south Korean national economy.

Under the pressure of U.S. monopoly capital and comprador capital, national industry in south Korea has been completely stifled and ruined. Owing to the increasing shortage of raw materials and funds and to the growing marketing difficulties, within just one year after the setting up of the military regime, industrial production fell by 9 percent.

South Korean agriculture has also been totally devastated. The vast peasant masses are still being harshly exploited under the feudalistic landlord system. Plunder and exploitation by the U.S. imperialists and the landlords have ruined south Korean agriculture severely. Both the total arable land and the area actually planted are steadily decreasing, and agricultural production is still based on backward, medieval techniques. Thus, south Korea, formerly a granary, has been converted into a region of chronic famine and has to import 4 to 5 million *sok* of U.S. surplus grain every year.

The south Korean people are living in untold misery due to economic bankruptcy on all fronts and cruel exploitation at the hands of the U.S. imperialists, the landlords, and the comprador capitalists.

Millions of working people have lost their jobs and are wandering in the streets. As no measures have been taken for their relief, they hover on the verge of starvation. Sixty percent of all the abled-bodied men in south Korea today are either unemployed or underemployed.

The people have been totally impoverished. Nevertheless, south Korea's rulers are exacting increasing taxes from the working people to cover their huge military expenditures. The tax burden on the south Korean people in 1962 increased 43 percent since 1960. As a result of the acute inflation caused by snowballing military spending, commodity prices are steadily rising. As of July this year, commodity prices in south Korea were up by more than 20 percent as against the end of 1960.

The U.S. imperialists have thoroughly disorganized the south Korean economy and brought unspeakable suffering to the south Korean people, transforming the whole of south Korea into a living hell where mass terror and tyranny prevail. The people's lives and property are constantly threatened by the American robbers, and our compatriots, our brothers and sisters are insulted and murdered by the aggressors. Mass starvation is sweeping south Korea, and almost every day many people starve to death.

This is the consequence of the colonial rule of U.S. imperialism in south Korea and of the traitorous policy of the south Korean rulers.

The only way to save the present ituation in south Korea and to relieve the people there from hunger and poverty is to drive out the U.S. troops and achieve national reunification.

Unless the complete independence and reunification of the country is achieved, the Korean people will not be able to live in peace for one minute, nor will the people in south Korea be able to free themselves from their present misery. The achievement of the great work of national reunification is the unanimous desire of all Koreans, in north and south. It is the supreme national task.

Reunification of our country should be achieved independently and by peaceful means without the interference of any outside forces after driving out foreign troops.

Having turned south Korea into their colony and military base and driven south Korean society into the depths of ruin, the U.S. imperialists are constantly threatening peace in Korea by aggravating tension. They are obstructing the reunification of our country by resorting to all sorts of sinister schemes.

The occupation of south Korea by the U.S. imperialists and their aggressive policy are the root causes of all the misfortunes and sufferings of the people in south Korea; they are the main obstacle to the progress of south Korean society and the peaceful reunification of our country.

History has never seen the achievement of independence and reunification when a country is occupied by foreign aggressor troops and is suffering outside interference.

Only by driving the U.S. army of aggression out of south Korea will it be possible to deliver the south Koreans from hunger, poverty, and colonial slavery, and to realize the national desire to reunify our divided country. Those who talk about the reunification of the country while justifying the occupation of south Korea by U.S. troops are, in fact, the opponents of reunification and agents of imperialism.

There is no reason whatsoever for the U.S. imperialists to station their troops in south Korea, nor can it be justified in any way. The U.S. army must pull out of south Korea and the Korean question must be settled by the Korean people themselves.

The U.S. imperialists are clamoring that the U.S. army must be stationed in south Korea in order to check "communist aggression from the north." But they can deceive no one with such a lie.

Our Party and the Government of the Republic are consistent in their efforts for the peaceful settlement of the Korean question. We have no intention of marching south, we have no intention of solving the question of Korean reunification by force of arms.

"Communist aggression from the north" is nothing but a subterfuge of the U.S. imperialists to cover up their sinister design to continue the occupation of south Korea, extend their invasion to the whole of Korea and further their aggression in Asia. The people in south Korea should thoroughly expose and frustrate the vicious scheming of the U.S. imperialists to invade all of Korea by pitting Koreans against Koreans.

We consider that the United Nations has no right to discuss the Korean question nor has it any right to meddle in the domestic affairs of our country. The Korean question should not be discussed by foreigners in New York or Washington; it should be discussed in Pyongyang or Seoul by the Koreans themselves.

The question of Korean reunification is an internal affair of the Korean people, and it can be settled by them alone. What grounds do foreign countries have for interfering in the domestic affairs of Korea, and how can they possibly settle the internal affairs of our nation? To try to achieve the reunification of the country by relying on outside forces is an illusion and is tantamount to leaving the whole of Korea open to imperialist aggression.

The Korean people can, and must reunify their country through their own efforts.

Reunification of our country is a complicated and difficult task that cannot be performed easily. Only through a hard and long-drawn-out struggle can we accomplish the great task of national reunification, for the U.S. imperialists, the overlords of world imperialism, have occupied south Korea and are now plotting frantically to unleash a new war, pursuing a policy of aggression against the whole of Korea and Asia.

We should carry out the independent, peaceful reunification of our country in a gradual way, through a series of intermediary steps, on the condition that foreign troops are withdrawn from south Korea.

In order to achieve the country's reunification, it is of paramount importance to eliminate the tension between north and south created by the U.S. imperialists.

The U.S. army should be withdrawn, a peace agreement should be concluded between the north and south on refraining from attack on each other and the armed forces of each be reduced to 100,000 or less. We have proposed this on a number of occasions and have done everything in our power to achieve this end.

Neither north nor south should increase their armed forces nor their armaments; instead, the armed forces should be reduced and tension eliminated so that both sides can work to build up the national economy and improve the living standards of the people.

The U.S. imperialists maintain a 700,000-strong mercenary army in south Korea, grinding the people down. This huge military force in the south has nothing to do with national defence; it is merely an instrument of U.S. imperialism for carrying out a policy of aggression. It imposes an unbearably heavy burden on the people in south Korea and seriously threatens peace in Korea.

The conclusion of a peace agreement between north and south Korea and the reduction of their respective armed forces would, above all, mean relief for the people in the south from the heavy burdens of military expenditure and removal of the tension that has been artificially created between north and south, thereby creating an atmosphere of mutual trust.

The withdrawal of all foreign troops from south Korea, the conclusion of a peace agreement between north and south, and the reduction of their armed forces would prove to be important initial steps towards the reunification of the country.

Elimination of tension between the north and south would enable us to take a further step and enter into economic and cultural exchange and co-operation.

A burning issue in south Korea today is the rehabilitation of its devastated economy and the improvement of the miserable living conditions of the people there. The only way of solving this problem is to establish economic and cultural relations and promote exchange and co-operation between the north and south.

Under the leadership of our Party, the people in the northern half have, through a heroic struggle, laid the foundations of industrialization and built a solid basis for an independent national economy. The economic foundations we have already established in the northern half of the Republic are a sure guarantee for the independent development of the national economy of Korea as a whole.

Only when economic co-operation and exchange between north and south Korea make it possible to take advantage of the economic foundations built in north Korea, can the industry and agriculture of south Korea be rehabilitated and developed, can the millions of unemployed be given jobs, and the life of its people generally improved.

We think it is necessary to organize an economic committee composed of representatives of north and south Korea for the purpose of effectively carrying out north-south exchanges.

The south Korean authorities, contrary to the will of the Korean people, are now trying to find a way out by bringing in foreign capital. The introduction of foreign capital leads to a state of dependence and national bankruptcy. This will only result in plunging the already ruined south Korean economy deeper into the abyss of hopeless destruction and in making south Korea more and more dependent on imperialism. The outcome of U.S. "aid" to south Korea over the 17 years since liberation is a striking proof of this.

When the north and the south combine their efforts to exploit our rich domestic resources, relying on the powerful economic foundations of north Korea, our nation will not only be able to stand on its own feet, but also build a modern, rich, powerful and independent state.

When exchange and mutual co-operation between the north and the south are put into effect, we shall be able to take another step towards epoch-making measures for the initial reunification of the country.

In order to achieve initial reunification, we consider the establishment of the Confederation already proposed by our Party and the Government of the Republic to be a reasonable step.

Our proposal of a Confederation is aimed at setting up a Supreme National Committee, composed of representatives of the Government of the Democratic People's Republic of Korea and the Government of the "Republic of Korea" to jointly solve matters of concern to the whole nation, while leaving intact the present socio-political systems in north and south Korea and ensuring the independence of action of the two governments.

Under the Confederation, neither north nor south shall interfere in the internal affairs of the other, nor shall one impose its will upon the other. North and south Korea shall act freely according to their respective political beliefs and jointly settle only those problems of common national interest on which agreement has been reached through the confederative body.

Unlike a confederation of nations with different languages, customs and cultures, the Confederation we propose would be a coming together of two temporarily divided parts of a single nation which has had the same language, customs and culture throughout its long history. Therefore, the establishment of the Confederation of north and south will make it possible for us to do tremendous work for a prosperity of the country and the benefit of the nation—developing the national economy and culture in a co-ordinated way and jointly exploiting all domestic resources, appearing as one nation in various fields of international activity, and so forth.

The establishment of the Confederation will also promote contacts and mutual understanding, strengthen politico-economic ties between north and south and create an atmosphere of national amity, thereby initiating a very favorable phase in the achievement of the complete peaceful reunification of our country.

We can, and must, achieve the complete reunification of our country by taking these intermediary steps.

As our Party and Government have made clear time and again, in order to achieve that goal, a unified central government, representing all strata of people in north and south Korea, must be set up on the basis of free elections throughout the whole country, conducted on democratic principles.

The guarantee of freedom to travel and freedom of political activity for the people both in north and south Korea, as well as the rejection of any interference by external forces, are prerequisites for free all-Korea elections.

In south Korea the suppression of the patriotic and democratic movement of the people must be brought to an end at once, and freedom of speech, the press, association and assembly, and freedom to demonstrate and to strike must be ensured. All political parties and social organizations outlawed by the military regime must be restored and complete freedom of their activities ensured.

All political parties, social organizations and individual public figures in north and south Korea must be guaranteed freedom of activity in all parts of the country and the freedom to express their political views before the people without any restriction whatsoever.

Only when these conditions are ensured can the Korean people establish an all-Korea central government through genuinely free elections and achieve the complete peaceful reunification of the country.

This stand of the Workers's Party of Korea and the Government of the Democratic People's Republic of Korea on the reunification of the country reflects the interests of the whole nation and the will of the entire Korean people.

Certain persons in south Korea are dead set against independent, peaceful reunification of our country, alleging that its realization would lead to the "communization" of south Korea. Whether the ideal of communism is realized in south Korea or not is a matter to be decided by the south Korean people themselves, and no one can impose it on them. No progressive ideas and social systems can be imposed from outside; they are chosen by people themselves of their own free will. To oppose the reunification of the country on the pretext of fearing the "communization" of south Korea is to go against the entire people's earnest desire for reunification and to betray the vital interests of the whole nation.

The rulers in south Korea still persist in their old "theory of wiping out communism for reunification" and are prattling on about building up their strength to "prevail over communism."

Attempts have already been made to wipe out communism and impose the colonial system on the whole of Korea through the power of imperialism, but this goal has proved absolutely unattainable. For almost 40 years, Japanese imperialist colonial rule could not stamp out the communist movement in Korea. Syngman Rhee who had made the extermination of communism his lifetime task could not achieve his goal even though banking on the power of U.S. imperialism. Rather he was forsaken by the people and met his downfall for his crimes. Some of those die-hards in south Korea who are bent on anti-communism must learn these lessons of history. Anyone daring to follow in the wake of Syngman Rhee will surely meet the same fate as his predecessor.

The reunification of our country is not a question of conquerors and conquered, but of the restoration of national unity in an originally united nation by completely freeing itself from the yoke of imperialism.

The pipe dream of "wiping out communism" or "prevailing over communism" is not only past all hope of realization. It is also a very harmful idea aimed at preventing the reunification of the country and perpetuating a divided nation.

The stand of our Party and the Government of the Republic on the reunification of the country is irrefutable; it is the most fair and reasonable one.

Anyone who truly defends the interests of the nation and is concerned about the future of the country should fight for an improved life for the people in south Korea, today in dire straits, and for the country's peaceful reunification. This is the solemn national duty of every Korean.

In order to achieve reunification of the country it is most important to promote mutual understanding, and achieve national amity and solidarity between north and south in every way. Antagonism and enmity between the north and south and the failure to achieve national unity only benefit the U.S. imperialists. The imperialist aggressors fear our national awakening and unity more than anything else. They resort to every vile scheme to undermine national unity, sow discord and create antagonism within the nation, with the object of achieving their goal of aggression.

All the patriotic people of north and south Korea should decisively smash the U.S. imperialist policy of dividing the nation and close ranks under the banner of national reunification.

We will unite and work together with anyone, regardless of his past record and political beliefs, as long as he defends the interests of the nation and works for the reunification of the homeland.

We can join hands even with those now in power in south Korea if they stop betraying the nation by conspiring with the foreign aggressors, stop repressing the people, and join in the struggle for independent, peaceful reunification of the country. But if they refuse to do so and continue to fawn upon the foreign forces and tag along behind them, repressing the people's just struggle for democracy and the right to live, and if they keep on obstructing the country's reunification to the last, it will be an indelible crime never to be erased from our nation's memory, and they will not be able to escape the stern judgment of the entire Korean people.

Unity should be achieved between the socialist forces of the northern half of the Republic and the patriotic, democratic forces of south Korea, and the whole nation should unite firmly in the fight against U.S. imperialist aggression and for the peaceful reunification of our country.

All sectors of the people in south Korea—workers, peasants, soldiers, youth and students, intellectuals and others—must rise up bravely in the save-the-nation struggle against the U.S. imperialist aggressors. The south Korean people must fight against the U.S. imperialist policy of aggression and war and determinedly reject any co-operation with the invader army. The south Korean people should put an end to the outrages committed by U.S. troops against our compatriots, our brothers and sisters, and wage a decisive struggle to force the aggressors out of our territory.

The south Korean people must fight both U.S. imperialism and the internal reactionary forces conspiring with it.

Under the banner of independent, peaceful reunification, the workers and peasants and all the patriotic, democratic forces of south Korea must form a broad united front for national salvation against U.S. imperialism; they must completely isolate the U.S. imperialists and the internal reactionary forces and prevent the reactionary rulers from relying on outside forces by constantly bringing pressure to bear on them.

We are living in a great era of national-liberation revolutions, when all the oppressed nations of the world are valiantly rising up to win their freedom and independence, casting aside the fetters of imperialism and colonialism. The spirit of struggle for national liberation is running high today in Asia, Africa and Latin America.

In such an era, how could our wise and courageous nation, which has a long history and culture of thousands of years and which has inherited the glorious revolutionary traditions, succumb to the oppression of Yankee imperialism and tolerate colonial slavery? All of us should rise up vigorously and intensify the flames of struggle for the reunification of the nation and the complete independence of the country, fighting U.S. imperialism and its accomplices, the reactionary ruling forces.

When the whole nation is firmly united and fighting a vigorous anti-U.S. save-the-nation struggle, the U.S. imperialist aggressors will finally be driven out of south Korea and the great task of national reunification will certainly be accomplished.

Reply To The Letter Of The President
Of the Korean Affairs Institute
In Washington

January 8, 1965

I have received your letter. It gives me great pleasure to learn that you are deeply concerned about the question of reunifying the country.

As you know, our nation has been a victim of territorial partition and national division for 20 years.

Although a new generation has grown up, there has not even been established contact and travel between north and south Korea, to say nothing of the reunification of the country, the long-cherished aspiration of the nation. The artificial barrier of national partition remains unchanged.

As the days go by, the gap between the north and the south is growing wider in all spheres of political, ecconomic and cultural life, and even the national characteristics common to our people, a homogeneous nation formed through a long history, are gradually becoming differentiated.

The division of the nation rules out the possibility of co-ordinated mobilization and use of the national wealth and the strength of the people for the development of the country; it brings unbearable suffering to all Korean people.

The division of Korea into north and south brings immeasurable miseries and misfortunes, particularly to the people's living in south Korea.

The prosperity of the whole nation cannot be expected and the people in south Korea cannot be rescued from their wretched plight unless the division of our country is terminated and reunification is achieved.

It is natural that in south Korea today, the broad masses of the people are crying out that they cannot live unless the country is reunified and many public figures with national conscience are fighting courageously for the reunification of the country.

Reunification of the country is an urgent national task which cannot be postponed any longer.

It is high time, we believe, for all Koreans without exception, who are patriotic and concerned about the future of the nation, to do their utmost to reunify the country.

The whole world knows that our Government, expressing the universal desire and will of the entire Korean people, has made persevering efforts to achieve the reunification of the country.

We consider that the solution of the reunification question must not be obstructed by the interests of any party, grouping or privileged circle at the expense of the national interests, and that reunification must in any case be accomplished in a democratic way, in accordance with the general will of the entire Korean people, and not by one side forcing its will on the other side. We do not allow anyone to impose their will upon us, and we, on our part, do not intend to force our will on others. We have always maintained that the authorities, political parties, social organizations and individual personalities of north and south Korea should sit down together and negotiate sincerely and open-heartedly to solve the question of reunification.

I make it clear once again that, just as we have done up to now, so in the future as well, our Government will exert every effort to achieve the reunification of the country in conformity with the desire of the people and the national interests, and that it is ready to accept anyone's opinion, if it is helpful toward the solution of the reunification question.

In your letter you set forth views that have many points in

common with a number of proposals we have already made time and again for the settlement of the question of reunifying the country.

As we have always maintained, the reunification of the country must be carried out in accord with the principles of independence and democracy, and in a peaceful way, without the interference of any outside forces.

We consider that any attempt to reunify the country by relying on outside forces is nothing but an illusion and is designed to leave the whole of Korea in the hands of the imperialist aggressors.

The question of Korean reunification is an internal affair of the Korean people which admits no interference from outside forces. The Korean question must be settled by the Koreans themselves. Foreigners are not in a position to solve the internal affairs of our nation.

Ours is a resourceful and civilized nation, fully capable of solving its national problem by itself.

The basic obstacle to the country's reunification is the U.S. imperialists who are occupying south Korea militarily, interfering in our domestic affairs, carrying out a policy of dividing our nation, and pursuing an aggressive policy against the whole of Korea.

The U.S. imperialists have brought south Korea completely under their colonial domination in all political, economic, military and cultural fields and brought utter ruin to the life of its people.

Withdrawal of all foreign troops from south Korea is the prerequisite to the solution of the question of reunification.

In north Korea there are abolutely no foreign troops. The Chinese People's Volunteers withdrew completely from north Korea on their own initiative as early as 1958.

However, the U.S. army in the guise of the United Nations is stationed in south Korea.

The United States has no ground or excuse whatsoever to station its army in south Korea.

There can be no independence or sovereignty as long as a foreign army of aggression is stationed on one's territory.

Any people who have the least spark of national conscience ought to demand the withdrawal of the U.S. troops and work to expel them from our territory.

We must stir up the indignation of the entire nation against the U.S. imperialist aggressors and mobilize all the partiotic forces in the struggle to drive the U.S. army out of south Korea.

Your proposal that all foreign troops should be withdrawn in order to solve the question of Korean reunification is a just one.

It is our consistent view that the question of Korean reunification should be solved through the establishment of a unified central government embracing representatives of people of all classes and strata, through free north-south general elections to be held in a democratic way, without interference by any outside forces, after the withdrawal of all foreign troops from south Korea.

Such general elections should be held in a completely free and democratic atmosphere, without any conditions that might hamper or repress, even slightly, the expression of the will of the people. Free, democratic elections are inconceivable as long as the democratic rights of the people are being violated and patriotic movements suppressed.

To hold free north-south general elections, there should first be full guarantees of complete freedom of political activity for all the political parties, social organizations and individual personalities, as well as freedom of speech, the press, assembly, association and demonstration, throughout north and south Korea. All the political prisoners who have been arrested and imprisoned for having demanded democratic liberties and the country's independent reunification should be set free unconditionally.

All citizens should have equal rights to elect and to be elected at any place throughout Korea, regardless of party affiliation, political views, property status, education, religious faith or sex.

Only through such genuinely democratic elections based on the principles of universal, equal and direct suffrage by secret ballot, can a unified independent and democratic government be established which represents the interests of the workers, peasants, youth and students, intellectuals, servicemen, traders, entrepreneurs and others from all classes and strata.

This proposal of ours is most fair and reasonable, acceptable to everyone.

However, the successive rulers of south Korea have doggedly opposed our just proposal, and have clamored for the so-called "elections under UN supervision."

The Korean people know only too well what "elections under UN supervision" are. It is no secret that the election of Syngman Rhee, traitor to the Korean people, was rigged up more than once, that Chang Myon's assumption to power was fabricated and the seizure of power by Pak Jung Hi was legalized, all through "elections under UN supervision" imposed on south Korea from 1948 to this date.

"Elections under UN supervision" are no more than a screen for covering the insidious aggressive plot of the U.S. imperialists to extend to north Korea the colonial system which they have forced upon the people in south Korea.

In Korea the United Nations has been used as an aggressive tool of the United States.

The United Nations has no competence whatsoever to involve itself in the Korean question.

The Korean people do not want anyone meddling in the solution of the question of their country's reunification. We must in any case achieve the reunification of the country by ourselves.

As the south Korean rulers, at the instigation of U.S. imperialism, persisted in opposing the establishment of a unified government of Korea through free, democratic elections, we could not merely sit with folded arms waiting for the day of reunification and could not but seek ways of gradual approach to complete reunification by taking all steps conducive to the reunification of the country.

You must know that we have long since been proposing the establishment of a Confederation of north and south Korea as a transitional step for settling the urgent and immediate problems of the nation even before the attainment of complete reunification of the country, and for facilitating reunification.

The Confederation we have proposed envisages the formation of a Supreme National Committee composed of equal numbers of representatives appointed by the two governments, mainly with the object of co-ordinating the economic and cultural development of north and south Korea in a unified way and of promoting mutual co-operation and exchange between the two sides in the common interests of the nation, while retaining the existing political systems in north and south Korea and maintaining the independent activities of the two governments.

The reunification commission you have suggested can be regarded as analogous to the Supreme National Committee we have mentioned. In our opinion, it would also be a good idea to work out measures for restoring the national bonds between the north and south and for carrying out the reunification of the country independently, not necessarily through the form of a Confederation, but by setting up some other kind of joint organ to be composed of representatices from north and south Korea.

We have maintained time and again that if the south Korean authorities cannot accept the Confederation, then the nation's tribulations caused by the division should at least be softened by effecting north-south economic and cultural exchange, leaving aside political questions for the time being.

The economic exchange between the north and the south would organically combine industrial north Korea with agrarian south Korea and facilitate the unified, independent development of the national economy, and would open the way for reviving south Korea's ruined economy and stabilizing the living conditions of its people who are in dire straits.

We have already built a developed industry and agriculture and laid firm economic foundations for an independent state in north Korea. This is the economic asset which would permit our nation to live independently after the country is reunified in the future.

When we were rebuilding, with tightened belts, the economy that had been ravaged beyond description by the U.S. imperialist aggressors, we were always mindful of the interests and future development of the whole nation. We have not for a moment forgotten our compatriots in south Korea; we consider it our sacred national duty to help the suffering people in south Korea.

Along with the carrying out of economic exchange, cultural ties in all spheres of science, culture, arts, sports, etc., should be restored, and travel of people between north and south should be effected.

The south Korean authorities, following the dictates of U.S. imperialism, are opposed to free north-south general elections, opposed to a Confederation of north and south Korea and opposed even to economic and cultural exchange and travel of people between north and south.

Under these circumstances, we insist that at least the exchange of letters should be materalized as a minimum step for forging ties between the north and south. This reflects the pressing demand of the people for ending the extremely abnormal situation in which parents, wives and children, relatives and friends who are separated in the north and the south cannot even write to each other.

It is of prime importance in achieving the reunification of the country to eliminate the tension created between the north and the south.

In this connection, it might be recalled, we have time and again proposed to the south Korean authorities that, after U.S. troops are completely withdrawn from south Korea, north and south Korean authorities conclude a peace agreement pledging not to resort to armed attack against each other, and that the armed forces of both north and south Korea be reduced to 100,000 or less.

The oversize armed forces of south Korea, numbering more than 600,000 men, are an unbearably heavy military expenditure for the south Korean people and severely menace peace in Korea.

The withdrawal of all foreign troops from south Korea, the conclusion of a peace agreement between the north and the south and the reduction of the armed forces on both sides will mark a giant step forward on the road to the country's reunification.

We regard as a welcome idea your proposal that the north and south Korean armies be cut to the level of constabulary units for the maintenance of internal security and order.

We are ready to take any other steps that may be helpful to the solution of the reunification question. We are willing to abrogate the military pacts we have concluded with foreign countries on the condition that the U.S. army is withdrawn from south Korea and the south Korean authorities abolish all the military pacts and agreements they have signed with foreign countries. We made this clear previously, when we were concluding the pacts with other countries.

Ours is an independent people's power established freely in accordance with the general will of the people. We have never relied on outside forces; we maintain complete independence in all spheres—political, economic, military and cultural.

Our domestic and foreign policies are completely independent, brooking no interference from any foreign country. Our Government, whenever it deems it necessary for the interests of the country and the nation, can take appropriate actions on its own initiative.

We have devoted all our sincere efforts to the reunification of our country.

Even after the present rulers of south Korea staged a military coup and seized power, we repeatedly advanced a number of proposals of national salvation aimed at removing the national calamity and accelerating the reunification of the country, in the sincere hope that they would return to a national position. However, following the aggressive and the divisive policy of the U.S. imperialists and disregarding the ardent desire of the nation, they have refused to listen to our sincere advice; on the contrary, they continue to perpetuate the partition of the nation.

The responsibility for the failure up to now to achieve the reunification of our country rests with the U.S. imperialists who have occupied south Korea by force of arms and have been pursuing a policy of splitting our nation, and with such traitors as Pak Jung Hi, the reactionary bureaucrats, the political quacks and impostors who, hand in glove with the U.S. imperialists, are bartering away the interests of the nation.

They serve the foreign aggressive forces, opposing the independent and peaceful reunification of the country and categorically rejecting the unity of the national forces; they defend only their own personal interests and those of some privileged circles that are in league with outside forces; they can never represent the south Korean people.

They defend, and ask for the permanent stationing of, the U.S. aggressive army which has occupied south Korea and has been obstructing the reunification of our country and perpetrating all and every kind of brutish atrocity such as plundering, oppressing, insulting and killing people in south Korea.

Those traitors, turning down our offer to receive millions of unemployed south Koreans into north Korea and give them jobs, are selling out our compatriots to European and American countries as if they were commodities.

Moreover, they are even ushering in the Japanese militarists to reduce south Korea to a colony of both U.S. and Japanese imperialism.

Manipulated by the United States, the traitors of south Korea, dead set against contact and co-operation within one and the same nation, are hurrying through the criminal "ROK-Japan talks" for collusion with the Japanese militarists.

Those taking the lead in conspiring with Japanese imperialism are the same stooges who served it faithfully in the past, too. Refusing to repent of their past crimes, they have now again become the cat's paw of U.S. imperialism and their old master, Japanese militarism.

To achieve the reunification of the country, we should pool the strength of the entire Korean people in north and south and fight against the foreign imperialist aggressive forces and their allies—the traitors, reactionary bureaucrats, political quacks and impostors who are hindering reunification.

How can we promote national unity and achieve the reunification of the country without fighting against those who, far from desiring reunification, categorically reject any contact or exchange between the north and south?

Needless to say, it would be a different matter if even now they were to repent of their mistakes and take the road of struggle for the withdrawal of the U.S. army and for the independent reunification of the country.

If a man defends the interests of the nation and desires the country's reunification, we will join hands and go together with him at any time, regardless of his political views and ideology and of his past record.

If all the patriotic forces of north and south Korea unite, we will definitely open the road to contact and negotiation between the north and the south, realize mutual co-operation and exchange, force the U.S. army to withdraw, and achieve the reunification of the country.

Without unity and struggle we can neither drive out the U.S. aggressor army nor achieve national reunification.

The point is that the south Korean people of all walks of life—workers, peasants, youth and students, intellectuals, armymen, traders, entrepreneurs, etc.—should firmly unite and wage a more resolute national-salvation struggle against U.S. imperialism and its stooges, for the independent and peaceful reunification of the country.

We should under no circumstances tolerate any form of interference in the domestic affairs of our nation; we must thoroughly oppose "protection" or "supervision" by any one and must carve out our own destiny by ourselves.

When we achieve the reunification of our country on the principle of the self-determination of nations and when the whole nation fights in unity, we will be able to increase the might of the country and build a rich and powerful, independent sovereign state, without needing "guarantees" from any outside forces.

Our country will surely be reunified through the nation-wide struggle of the entire Korean people.

In conclusion, I express the hope that you will make positive efforts to accelerate the independent reunification of the country.

Let Us Embody the Revolutionary Spirit of Independence, Self-Sustenance and Self-Defence More Thoroughly in All Fields of State Activity *(Excerpt)*

Political Program of the Government of the Democratic People's Republic of Korea Announced at the First Session of the Fourth Supreme People's Assembly of the D.P.R.K., December 16, 1967

First. The Government of the Republic will thoroughly implement the line of independence, self-sustenance and self-defence to consolidate the political independence of the country, further strengthen the foundations of an independent national economy capable of ensuring the complete reunification, independence and prosperity of our nation, and increase the defence capabilities of the country so as to reliably safeguard its security on the basis of our own forces, by excellently materializing our Party's idea of *Juche* in all fields.

Our Party's idea of *Juche* represents the most correct Marxist-Leninist idea of leadership for the successful accomplishment of our revolution and construction and is the invariable guiding principle of the Government of the Republic in all its policies and activities.

Only by firmly establishing *Juche* can each country repudiate flunkeyism to great powers and dogmatism and creatively apply

111

the universal truth of Marxism-Leninism and the experience of other countries in line with its historical conditions and national characteristics; always solve its own problems by itself on its own responsibility, eliminating reliance on others while displaying the spirit of self-reliance; and, accordingly, carry on its revolutionary cause and construction work successfully.

Establishing *Juche* is a question of special importance for us in the light of our country's geographical situation and environment, the specifics of its historical development and the complex and arduous character of our revolution. The establishment of *Juche* is a question of key importance on which the success of our revolution depends, a vital question which will determine the future of our nation.

The Government of the Republic has been able to score great victories and successes in the revolutionary struggle and construction work, as it has persistently endeavoured to solve all problems independently, in conformity with the specific realities of our country and mainly through its own efforts, guided consistently by the *Juche* idea of the Workers' Party of Korea in its activities and strictly adhering to the principles of Marxism-Leninism.

As a result of our efforts to establish *Juche* in the ideological field, the national pride of our workers and their sense of independence have grown tremendously, and they have acquired these revolutionary characteristics: not following others blindly, approaching foreign things critically instead of mechanically copying or swallowing them whole; and striving to solve all problems according to the actual conditions of our country and on the basis of their own wisdom and strength.

Thanks to the fact that our Party's spirit of independence, self-sustenance and self-defence is finding full expression in all fields of national construction, the political independence of the Republic has been consolidated and the economic independence and military power of our country have grown even more.

As a full-fledged, independent state, our country now sets its own lines and policies independently and exercises complete equality and sovereignty in its foreign relations.

Under the leadership of our Party and the Government of the

Republic, our people have laid firm foundations for an independent national economy in accord with the revolutionary principle of self-reliance and thus eliminated the centuries-old backwardness and poverty, further increased the economic might of the Republic and radically improved their standard of living. The establishment of *Juche* in science and culture has accelerated scientific and technological progress, brought about a great qualitative change in education and in the work of training cadres, and led to the blossoming and advancement of a new, socialist national culture congenial to the life and sentiments of our people.

In the field of defence construction, too, we have strengthened our defence capabilities to such an extent that we are in a position to firmly defend the security of our country and our socialist gains, even in the complex situation existing today, on the basis of our own strength.

The great victories and successes we have attained in our socialist revolution and socialist construction over the past years are, indeed, the brilliant fruition of the great vitality of our Party's idea of *Juche* and of our line of independence, self-sustenance and self-defence—the embodiment of that idea in all fields. We formulated our policies independently by creatively applying the principles of Marxism-Leninism to the specific realities of Korea and enlisted the inexhaustible creative potential of our industrious and talented people and our rich national resources to carry out these policies. This has enabled us to build a socialist state in a short time, which has political independence, economic self-sustenance and national self-defence.

Our Party's line of strengthening the political, economic and military might of the country in every way with all our efforts is the most correct way of expediting the victory of the Korean revolution.

The Government of the Republic will continue to adhere firmly to the principle of settling independently all the problems that arise in revolution and construction, studying and analysing the realities of Korea in strict accordance with the *Juche* idea of the Workers' Party of Korea.

All nations are equal and have the solemn right of national self-determination, of deciding their own destinies for themselves. A nation can secure independence and freedom and attain welfare and prosperity only if it achieves complete political self-determination and exercises its rights, taking them firmly into its hands.

Under the leadership of our Party, the Government of the Republic will use its own head in formulating all our policies for socialist construction in the fields of industry, agriculture, education, literature and art, judicial administration, etc., in conformity with our realities, and carry them out with its own efforts. We must not act on orders and instructions of others but, on the basis of the interests of our revolution and construction, settle all problems from the standpoint of *Juche*, using our own judgment and making our own decisions. It is true that we should unite with friends who are fighting for a common goal and learn from their experience if it accords with the principles of Marxism-Leninism, and it is worth learning. But even so, we must always approach such experience critically, vehemently opposing the tendency to swallow foreign things whole or imitate them mechanically; we must not blindly copy what does not fit our actual conditions.

In the struggle for our country's reunification, too, the Government of the Republic will always hold fast to its independent position. We regard all attempts to effect the country's reunification by relying on outside forces as treacheries against the country and the nation, aimed at placing the whole of Korea in the hands of foreign aggressors. The question of Korean reunification is an internal affair of the Korean people, one which cannot be settled by any outside forces. Ours is a wise and civilized nation, fully capable of settling its national problems for itself. We consistently hold that the question of reunifying our country must be settled through the efforts of our people themselves, without interference from any outside forces, under the condition that the aggressive army of U.S. imperialism is withdrawn from south Korea.

In the sphere of foreign policy, too, we should continue to work to establish political and economic relations with other countries on the principles of complete equality and mutual respect. We must always rely on our own judgment and conviction in struggling against imperialism and Right and "Left" opportunism, in conformity with our actual conditions, and let no one violate and affront the rights and dignity of our nation.

The Government of the Republic will continue to faithfully carry out our Party's line of building an independent national economy by fully applying the principle of self-reliance in the economic sphere, while, at the same time, consolidating political independence.

Today we are confronted with the weighty task of carrying on economic construction and defence upbuilding in parallel, to lay a firm material foundation for the prosperity of all the generations to come and establish a sound economic base which will enable us to readily cope with the great revolutionary event of the reunification of our country. All this can be achieved successfully only if the principle of self-reliance, the line of building an independent national economy is adhered to consistently and implemented more thoroughly.

Self-reliance is a thoroughly revolutionary stand for a people to accomplish the revolution in their country mainly relying on their own forces; it is an independent stand of building up their country through their own labor and with their own national resources.

Only by firmly maintaining such a revolutionary stand and revolutionary principle can we carry on the struggle without forsaking revolutionary constancy, no matter what complex and difficult situation may confront us, and assure victory in the revolutionary struggle and success in our work of construction, bravely overcoming difficulties and hardships that stand in the way of our advance. If you lack the revolutionary spirit of self-reliance, you may lose faith in your own strength, neglect efforts to tap the inner resources of your country, grow indolent and loose, and fall into a state of passivity and conservatism.

Only when a nation builds an independent national economy can it secure political independence, make its country rich, strong and advanced, and achieve national prosperity.

Economic independence is the material foundation for political independence. A country which is economically dependent on outside forces becomes a political satellite of other countries; an economically subjected nation cannot free itself from colonial slavery politically.

Without building an independent national economy it is impossible to establish material and technological foundations for socialism, and build socialism and communism successfully.

To build socialism, it is essential to create a powerful base of heavy industry with the machine-building industry as its core, and, on this basis, equip light industry, agriculture, transport and all other branches of the national economy with up-to-date techniques, thus laying the powerful material and technological foundations for socialism—needed to improve the welfare of the working people as a whole—as the laws of socialism require.

As long as national distinctions remain and states exist, these material and technological foundations of socialism must be built by each national state as a unit. Therefore, it can be said that firm material and technological foundations of socialism have been laid in each country only when it has built a comprehensive, independent national economy diversified in its development, equipped with the latest technology and run by its own national cadres, using its own natural resources, raw materials and other supplies so that its domestic products can fully meet the varied and ever-growing requirements of economic and defence construction and the people's consumption, for heavy and light industrial goods and farm produce.

Only if the material and technological foundations of socialism are established in this way within the bounds of each national state as a comprehensive, independent economic unit, can the country's natural resources be tapped and utilized to the fullest and a high rate of growth in production be maintained together with a correct and flexible balance among all branches of the national economy. Moreover, only in this way is it possible to develop science, technology and culture rapidly, steadily raise the technological and cultural standards of the working people, and turn them into people of a new type, developed in an all-round way.

The building of an independent national economy is also the

basic guarantee that nations can eliminate the economic backwardness which constitutes the real basis of inequalities between them, achieve national prosperity and build a socialist and communist society successfully.

The building of a socialism and communism, as you know, requires the eradication of inequalities between nations as well as of class distinctions.

Such inequalities, however, do not disappear immediately when the socialist revolution triumphs in each country, nor do they vanish through the amalgamation of nations in one way or another.

The era of capitalism is an era in which national oppression prevails side by side with class exploitation, an era in which the free development of the great majority of nations is held back by a few nations and inequalities between nations exist. It is, therefore, necessary for the nations liberated from capitalist exploitation and oppression not only to become laboring socialist nations but also to build highly developed, independent national economies for their fullest free development and all-round efflorescence. Only by so doing can all inequalities among nations be done away with and can all nations build socialism with success, and gradually go on to communism.

All this testifies to the fact that the line of building an independent national economy, consistently followed by our Party and the Government of the Republic, is a thoroughly revolutionary line of economic construction that conforms with the laws which govern the building of socialism and communism.

We will apply the revolutionary principle of self-reliance in building up our national defences as well, and thus further increase our country's capabilities for self-defence.

Needless to say, the international unity of the proletariat of all countries and the friendly alliance of the socialist countries in the revolutionary struggle against imperialist aggression and against the pressures of international capital are an important guarantee for safeguarding the revolutionary gains already obtained and winning new victories. It is the sacred internationalist duty of Communists to do all they can to help and give support and encouragement to each other in the battle against imperialism, their common enemy, and each country should strive to strengthen this international solidarity in the struggle against imperialist forces of aggression from without.

The decisive factor for victory in the struggle against imperialist reaction, however, is the internal forces of the country concerned. Although foreign support is important in a war against foreign aggressors, to all intents and purposes it plays no more than a secondary role. When the internal forces in a country are not prepared, its revolutionary struggle cannot emerge victorious, no matter how great its foreign support may be. If the Communists only pin their hopes on foreign support and aid, without developing their own revolutionary forces, they cannot be sure of defending the security of their country and their revolutionary gains against imperialist aggression.

The Government of the Republic will materialize our Party's spirit of self-defence, thoroughly preparing our people and soldiers politically and ideologically for war; it will make full material preparations to defend out country, relying on the solid foundations of the independent national economy we have already established and, at the same time, further increase our military might.

Particularly, by carrying out the decisions of the Conference of the Workers' Party of Korea in full, we will concentrate all our efforts on reorganizing the whole work of building our socialist economy to fit the requirements of the present situations and on reinforcing our defence capabilities to meet the undisguised aggressive manoeuvres by the enemy. Thus, we will make ours an ever more solid and viable, independent economy to fully meet the material needs of both the front lines and the rear in case of emergency, and we will make our country's military power impregnable to repel the enemy on our own no matter when he may launch a surprise attack against us.

Materializing the *Juche* idea of the Workers' Party of Korea successfully in all fields, we will build an ever richer, stronger and mightier socialist state—independent in politics, self-sustaining in the economy and self-defensive in national defence.

Second. In order to end the present misfortunes of our people caused by the artificial split of our territory and nation as soon as possible, liberate the people in south Korea and reunify our country, the Government of the Republic will firmly equip the people in the northern half morally and materially to always support the south Korean people in their sacred anti-U.S. struggle for national salvation and to readily cope with the great revolutionary event.

Because of the occupation of south Korea by the U.S. imperialists, our country is still divided into north and south, and the reunification of the country, the heartfelt desire of the nation, has not yet been achieved even though a new generation has grown up. Our people have been suffering from the national split for more than 20 years. As the days go by, the gulf between north and south Korea is widening in all spheres— political, economic and cultural—and the national community of our people, formed through a long history, is gradually melting away. Territorial partition and national split make it impossible to co-ordinate our efforts to enlist and utilize our country's wealth and national wisdom and talents to promote the prosperity of the country and the welfare of the people.

The division of Korea into north and south has caused immeasurable misery and distress particularly to the south Korean people. South Korea today has been completely turned into a colony of the U.S. imperialists, into their military base of aggression. The national industry of south Korea has been reduced to dependency on foreign capital, and its agriculture, too, is in serious crisis. The national culture and the beautiful customs inherent in the Korean people have been utterly trampled underfoot, and all kinds of immorality and depravity prevail everywhere in south Korea. The south Korean people are going hungry, in rags, doubly and triply exploited and oppressed, many of them roaming the streets in quest of work and living in a state of constant anxiety with all hopes blighted. They are subjected to unbearable racial insults and contempt, and even their right to existence is constantly threatened by the U.S. imperialist aggressors.

Where there are exploitation and oppression, there will always be revolutionary struggle on the part of the people. Ever since the first days of the occupation of the southern half by the U.S. imperialist aggressors, the south Korean people have been fighting tenaciously against their policies of colonial enslavement and military aggression. The October Popular Resistance Struggle in 1946, the April Uprising in 1960 which toppled the puppet regime of Syngman Rhee, and many struggles waged successively by the south Korean people against the "ROK-Japan talks" and for the abrogation of the "ROK-Japan agreements," dealt telling blows to the colonial rule of U.S. imperialism.

Each time, the U.S. imperialists and their stooges harshly repressed the people's righteous patriotic struggle at the point of the bayonet. The policy of military fascist dictatorship pursued in south Korea today has assumed unprecedented ferocity and barbarity and has become a prototype of vicious fascist rule by the imperialists over their colonies. The U.S. imperialist aggressors and their puppets, while manufacturing numerous wicked fascist laws, greatly increased their repressive apparatuses, and covered the whole of south Korea with military, police, intelligence and special agent networks, thereby turning it into a living hell of terrorism and murder.

In south Korea today the U.S. imperialists and the Pak Jung Hi clique are intensifying their fascist repression to the limit. Everywhere they are making all sorts of frenzied attempts to repress the south Korean people, who are fighting harder than ever for the right to live, for democratic liberties and for the reunification of their country. According to south Korean press reports, this year alone ten or more division including U.S. imperialist troops, south Korean puppet army, police forces, and reserve divisions, were mobilized to crush the actions of armed groups of south Korean revolutionaries and the mass revolutionary struggles, breaking out one after another all over south Korea. A total of more than six million U.S. imperialist troops, south Korean puppet troops and police took part directly in the so-called "mopping-up operations." The U.S. imperialists and the Pak Jung Hi clique cruelly suppressed the revolutionary organization formed around Dr. Kim Dae Su, professor at Kyongbuk University, arresting and imprisoning more than ten patriotic intellectuals. Last autumn they arrested many young people in and around Pusan on the charge of involvement in the alleged case of the People's Revolutionary Party. Again, they recently used trumped-up charges in what they called the "case of the Operative Group for the Communization of South Korea" in Seoul and, on the other hand, arrested and imprisoned many university professors, other intellectuals and patriotic figures, branding the Society for Comparative Studies on Nationalism—an academic organization—as a "seditious organization," and tried the victims in a kangaroo court. They have thus committed the heinous crime of "demanding" the death penalty or life imprisonment for many innocent persons.

They are raising an ever louder "anti-communist" hue and cry under the nonsensical allegation that all the fierce revolutionary struggles of the patriotic people which are breaking out all over south Korea today are the work of "spies" sent down from north Korea; and they are trying hard to take the minds of the south Korean people off their troubles and to deceive the peoples of the world.

But no amount of brutal repression and "anti-communist" campaign by the U.S. imperialists and the Pak Jung Hi puppet clique can ever dampen the indomitable revolutionary fighting spirit of the south Korean people or block their sweeping revolutionary advance. Today broad sections of the south Korean people are waging a vigorous struggle in all fields, holding still higher the banner of anti-U.S. resistance struggle for national salvation. A people can win freedom and liberation only through its own struggle. When the broad masses of the people rise as one in a struggle against their oppressors, they can destroy any imperialist bulwark. If the workers and peasants, youth and students, intellectuals and other broad sectors of the people in south Korea unite firmly and come out courageously in revolutionary struggle, they will be able to deal a crushing defeat to the U.S. imperialists and the Pak Jung Hi clique and accomplish the cause of the south Korean revolution.

On behalf of the entire people in the northern half of the Republic, I send warm revolutionary greetings to the revolutionaries and democratic figures, to all the patriotic people who are putting up a valiant struggle in various parts of south Korea, underground, in mountains, and even in prison.

All the people in the northern half of the Republic bear the great responsibility of carrying the south Korean revolution to a conclusion, giving active support to the struggle of the south Korean people, keeping up with their exalted fighting spirit.

As long as the U.S. imperialists continue to occupy south Korea and our country remains partitioned, the Korean people cannot live in peace even for a moment and the people in south Korea cannot extricate themselves from their present misery and pain. The occupation of south Korea by U.S. imperialism and its policy of aggression are the source of all the misfortunes of our nation and the main obstacle to the reunification of our country.

We cannot simply contemplate the miserable plight of our south Korean compatriots with folded arms and we can never bequeath a divided country to our descendants. As long as this wretched situation continues in which the country and the nation are divided and our compatriots, blood brothers and sisters, are subjected to all sorts of racial insults and ill treatment by the foreign aggressors, no Korean Communist or conscientious Korean nationalist can say that he has fulfilled his duty.

We must accomplish the south Korean revolution and reunify the country in our generation and bequeath a unified country to the new generations. We must prepare all necessary conditions for the reunification of our country as soon as possible.

The accomplishment of the great cause of liberating south Korea and reunifying the country at the earliest possible date depends not only on how the revolutionary organizations and revolutionaries in south Korea expand and strengthen the revolutionary forces and how they fight the enemy but also, to a large extent, on how the people in the northern half of the Republic prepare themselves to cope with the great revolutionary event.

The most important thing in completing the south Korean revolution and hastening the reunification of the country is to well prepare all our people politically and ideologically and, at the same time, create all the necessary material conditions.

We should always give active material and moral support and

encouragement to the south Korean people in their anti-U.S., national-salvation struggle and consider the south Korean revolution and the reunification of the country our first and foremost revolutionary task. We can never allow ourselves to become self-complacent with the achievements wrought in the northern half and become lax and indolent. How can we sit idly by at a time when the south Korean people, suffering from hunger, are waging a struggle at the cost of their blood? It is our lofty national duty and the supreme task of the nation to force the U.S. imperialist aggressors out of our territory, liberate south Korea and reunify our country by pooling our strength with that of the south Korean people.

The people in the northern half of the Republic should always remember their brothers in the south and have revolutionary determination to liberate them at all costs. They should be firmly prepared ideologically to be mobilized for a decisive struggle to accomplish the cause of the reunification of the country by joining forces with the south Korean people whenever called upon to go to their aid, as the struggle of the people surges forward and the revolutionary situation ripens in south Korea.

Meanwhile, socialist economic construction, the principal guarantee for strengthening the material forces of our revolutionary base, should be successfully carried on to further consolidate the economic foundations of our country so that adequate material preparations can be made to support the revolutionary struggle of the south Korean people and to readily cope with the great revolutionary event of realizing the reunification of our country.

The present situation requires us to conduct all our work in a more active, more revolutionary manner. We must subordinate everything to the struggle to accomplish the south Korean revolution by giving support to the south Korean people in their struggle and to reunify our country.

The northern half of the Republic is the revolutionary base for accomplishing the great cause of national liberation throughout the country, and its revolutionary forces are the most important motive power for the Korean revolution as a whole. All the working people should fully realize that, unless the revolutionary base of the northern half of the Republic is fortified and its revolutionary forces are strengthened still more, it will be impossible to give positive support to the south Korean revolution and achieve the reunification of our country. They must continue to wage a tenacious struggle on all fronts of socialist economic construction and produce and build more, better and cheaper with our existing manpower, equipment and materials by discovering and activating reserves and potentialities to the utmost. All functionaries and working people, as masters in their country, should assiduously manage all aspects of economic life, both national and individual, and make every effort not to waste a single grain of rice, a single gram of iron or a single drop of gasoline.

Only when our country's economic foundations are more consolidated and the necessary material conditions are sufficiently created can we cope with the great event with full preparations, bring the superiority of the socialist system home to the fighting people of south Korea and give powerful support to their revolutionary struggle. Only then will it be possible to create assets with which to put the devastated south Korean economy back on its feet and rapidly improve the deteriorated living conditions of the people in the southern half, after the reunification of the country.

All our functionaries and working people should work like masters, and live frugally, with a great revolutionary zeal, in the lofty spirit of supporting the south Korean people more actively in their anti-U.S., national-salvation struggle and of expediting the revolutionary cause of the reunification of the country. We can never get complacent and lax nor countenance the slightest laziness, immorality or luxury. We are making a revolution and we should work and live in a revolutionary way, ready and alert at all times.

All our people will, in this way, be made to readily cope with the great revolutionary event of national reunification. We should all be ready and willing to take part in the revolutionary struggle whenever called upon to do so by the Party.

Report to the Fifth Congress of the Workers' Party of Korea on the Work of the Central Committee *(Excerpt)*

November 2, 1970

For the South Korean Revolution and the Reunification of our Country

Comrades, the south Korean revolution is a component part of the Korean revolution as a whole. To achieve the victory of the Korean revolution on a nation-wide scale, it is essential to push forcefully ahead with socialist construction in the northern half of the Republic and, at the same time, further advance the revolutionary struggle in south Korea.

The period under review has witnessed tremendous changes in the south Korean situation. The U.S. imperialists have more completely reduced south Korea to a military base of aggression, their military appendage, and pushed their policies of aggression and war harder than ever through a fascist military dictatorship. On the other hand, national and class contradictions have become more acute in south Korea and the revolutionary advance of the workers, peasants and other broad sectors of the people has been stepped up. As a consequence U.S. imperialism's colonial rule has gone into a deeper crisis. These are the main developments which occurred in south Korea over the past period.

The south Korean revolution is a national-liberation revolution against the U.S. imperialist aggressors and, at the same time, a people's democratic revolution against the stooges of U.S. imperialism—the landlords, comprador capitalists and reactionary bureaucrats—and their fascist rule. The basic task of this revolution is to drive the U.S. imperialist forces of aggression out of south Korea, get rid of their colonial domination, and overthrow the fascist military dictatorship in order to establish a progressive social system, thus developing south Korean society democratically.

The U.S. imperialists are the real rulers who have seized all power in south Korea. They are the first target of the south Korean revolutionary struggle. The occupation of south Korea by U.S. imperialism and its colonial rule is the basic cause of all the misery and pains the south Korean people are suffering. Until the U.S. imperialist aggressors are forced out of south Korea and their colonial rule is smashed, the south Korean people cannot escape their present wretched plight. The tiny handful of landlords, comprador capitalists and reactionary bureaucrats in south Korea faithfully execute the aggressive policy of the U.S. imperialists and, under their patronage, cruelly oppress and exploit the people.

The motive power of the south Korean revolution is the working class and its dependable ally, the peasantry, and the progressive student youth, intellectuals, patriotic-minded soldiers and some patriotic national capitalists and petty bourgeoisie who are opposed to U.S. imperialism and its lackeys.

The revolutionary struggle in south Korea is a just struggle of these and other sectors of the people against the U.S. imperialist forces of aggression and their accomplices—the landlords, comprador capitalists and reactionary bureaucrats.

From liberation to the present, the south Korean people have kept up an unflagging revolutionary struggle against U.S. imperialism and its underlings.

The revolutionary struggle of the south Korean people has gradually entered a new stage of development, especially in the postwar years, and hewed its way, despite harsh trials, to greater successes. After the war the south Korean people—inspired by the achievements in socialist revolution and construction in the northern half—fought on staunchly against U.S. imperialism and its stooges, for political freedom, democratic rights and the reunification of the country.

In the course of this struggle, the south Korean revolutionaries and the people have shed much blood and suffered a number of heart-rending setbacks. But their sacrifices and failures have not been in vain. This has gradually made them grasp a valuable truth of revolutionary struggle: the ferocious enemy can be defeated only with an organized force.

The south Korean revolutionaries keenly felt the need to build a party to unite the revolutionary forces into one solid block and to give co-ordinated leadership to the struggle, and they strove to make that materialize. As a result of their untiring struggle and as a reflection of the essential requirements of the development of the south Korean revolutionary movement, the Progressive Party, a legal political party of the south Korean revolutionaries, came into being in December 1955.

The Progressive Party put forward a fighting program with anti-imperialism, anti-fascism and peaceful reunification as its key points and launched an active struggle to rally patriotic democratic forces in various strata, opposing the policies of national division and fascistization pursued by U.S. imperialism and its henchmen. The Progressive Party acquired increased prestige among broad segments of the south Korean people and the peaceful reunification program advanced by the Party especially enjoyed strong support from the south Korean public. This was unquestionably testified during the puppet presidential "election" in 1956, when the Progressive Party "candidate" won more than 2 million votes, or slightly less than what was raked up by Syngman Rhee, loyal ballcarrier for U.S. imperialism—and this despite the outrageous repression, fraud and swindling on the part of U.S. imperialism and its stooges. This graphically showed that the south Korean people were against the fascist colonial rule of U.S. imperialism and its policy of national division and fervently desired the peaceful reunification of our country and democratic social development. The U.S. imperialists and their henchmen were so terrified by the rapidly expanding and increasing influence of the Progressive Party among the south Korean people that they launched bloody repression, perpetrating the bestial barbarity of arresting and imprisoning numerous members of the Progressive Party and slaying its leader Mr. Cho Bong Am. They forcibly dissolved the Party and it ceased to exist in January 1958. Though the Progressive Party failed to transform the fighting spirit of the south Korean people into a mass revolutionary movement against the enemy and even to take effective action to preserve its own revolutionary forces, it gave a considerable impetus to the trend toward national reunification in south Korea and to the development of the anti-U.S., anti-dictatorship struggle of the people.

After the dissolution of the Progressive Party, the U.S. imperialists and their stooges further stepped up their repression of the south Korean patriots. In spite of all hardships and trials, however, the dynamic revolutionary struggle of the people went on without letup and the revolutionary forces grew steadily in south Korea.

The Popular Uprising of April 1960 marked a new turning point in the advancement of the south Korean revolutionary movement. The April Popular Uprising was an explosion of the enmity and resentment of the south Korean people which had long been pent up under the colonial rule of U.S. imperialism and its lackeys. It was a mass resistance struggle against the U.S. and for national salvation, involving millions of the broad masses throughout south Korea. The puppet government of Syngman Rhee, veteran lackey of U.S. imperialism, was finally overthrown by the heroic struggle of the masses of the south Korean people, including student youth and intellectuals. This was the first victory won after the war by the south Korean people in their anti-U.S. national-salvation struggle. The April Popular Uprising clearly demonstrated the heroic mettle of the south Korean people and proved that if the masses pool their strength and rise in a struggle against the oppressors, they can certainly crush any enemy stronghold. With the April 19 Uprising the crisis of the colonial rule of U.S. imperialism deepened in south Korea, and the situation turned in favor of the revolution.

Following the April Popular Uprising, the revolutionary advance of the patriots and the masses of south Korea intensified with each passing day and progressive political forces appeared on the scene. In this process the Socialist Mass Party came into being. Under the guidance of the south Korean revolutionaries the Socialist Mass Party set forth, as its immediate task, the founding of a unified democratic state based on the line of national independence, and conducted brisk organizational and political activities aimed at leading a massive advance of the people in a national-salvation movement for the independent reunification of our country. The Party formed the "Central Council for Independent National Reunification," a united-front coalition of the broad democratic forces, and organized and directed the joint struggle of all strata of the people against U.S. imperialism and its lackeys. Under the leadership of the Socialist Mass Party the fierce flames of struggle enveloped the whole of south Korea. The student youth and people there waged a heroic fight to tear down the barrier between north and south, with slogans like "Reunification is the only way out," "Let's go north, come south, let's meet at Panmunjom!"

The Socialist Mass Party, however, was not able to develop the revolutionary advance of the student youth into a struggle that would end the occupation of south Korea by U.S. imperialism, smash its colonial ruling machine and establish a democratic government; nor could it organize the workers, peasants and other sectors of the broad masses, and mobilize them in the struggle. When the U.S. imperialists instigated the reactionary military gangsters to stage a counterrevolutionary "military coup" and make a fascist attack on the revolutionary forces, the Socialist Mass Party failed to deal a resolute counterstroke, and in the end the struggle of the students was suppressed.

After the May 16 "military coup" the U.S. imperialists and their stooges launched into naked fascist military rule in south Korea. They trampled on even the elementary democratic free-

doms and rights of the south Korean people and forcibly dissolved all progressive political parties and social organizations,
closed down organs of the press and perpetrated such bar-
barities as the wholesale arrest, imprisonment and slaughter of
hundreds of thousands of revolutionaries and patriotic people.
The Socialist Mass Party was thus destroyed by brutal repression on the part of the enemy, and the revolutionary forces of
south Korea suffered heavy losses.

But the revolutionaries and patriotic people of south Korea
were further awakened and acquired many valuable lessons and
precious experience in this postwar process of struggle. The
historical experience of the south Korean revolutionary movement has clearly proved that there can be no peaceful transition
in the struggle for power and that no revolution can be led to
victory by a mass movement alone. Under the patronage of U.S.
imperialism, the successive reactionary rulers of south Korea
cold-bloodedly slaughtered progressive figures backed by the
people when there appeared even the slightest likelihood of
their assumption of power. Every mass movement of the people
for national reunification against U.S. imperialist colonial rule
was answered with barbarous repression. The Progressive Party
was crushed as soon as it gained popularity in the elections with
its slogan of national reunification, and the Socialist Mass Party
was also forcibly dissolved when it led the broad masses in the
national-salvation struggle for the reunification of our country
and won high prestige among the people. It is usual for the
enemy to resort to terrorism against those who are inclined to
take a revolutionary stand for the sake of their country and
nation. Shortly after liberation, the enemy assassinated Mr. Ryo
Un Hyong simply because he had advocated the peaceful
reunification of the country. They also assassinated Mr. Kim Gu
when he turned progressive after attending the Joint Conference of Representatives of the North and South Korean Political
Parties and Social Organizations. The revolutionaries and patriotic people in south Korea came to realize more keenly that
they could win power only through revolutionary struggle,
since the reactionary south Korean rulers would not meekly
relinquish their ruling power but were desperately resorting to

counterrevolutionary violence to stifle the progressive forces. They drew from this the priceless lesson that, in order to win victory for the revolution, they had to be fully prepared to resist the enemy's counterrevolutionary violence with revolutionary violence, while waging an active mass struggle for democratization against fascism.

The April 19 Popular Uprising and subsequent developments, in particular, taught an important lesson: that the people could win their democratic freedoms and rights only through a decisive revolutionary struggle to drive the U.S. imperialist aggressors out of south Korea and overthrow the colonial rule of U.S. imperialism and that this struggle would emerge victorious only when the broad masses of the people, including workers, peasants and student youth, were mobilized under the leadership of a Marxist-Leninist Party, the vanguard detachment of the working class.

Drawing on the valuable experiences and lessons acquired at the cost of blood in their struggle against the enemy, the south Korean revolutionaries have devoted their all to developing the revolutionary struggle in defiance of cruel repression by the fascist military rulers. In the establishment of a Marxist-Leninist Party of the working class they found the key to over-coming the most serious weaknesses of the previous revolutionary movements in south Korea and to advancing the revolution successfully. They hastened the building of the Revolutionary Party for Reunification in the face of great hardships and difficulties.

As a united Marxist-Leninist Party, a party of the working class, the Revolutionary Party for Reunification was born in the hard revolutionary fight of the south Korean revolutionaries and people against the U.S. imperialists and their stooges. With its emergence, broad masses of the oppressed and exploited people in south Korea have acquired a genuine defender of their class and national interests. The south Korean people today have a reliable political general staff in their revolutionary battle for freedom and liberation.

The political stand and the fighting goals of the Revolutionary Party for Reunification are explicitly stated in its Manifesto and Programme, made public in the name of its Central Committee in Seoul in August of last year.

The Manifesto and the Programme of the Revolutionary Party for Reunification emphasized that the guiding idea of the Party is the Marxist-Leninist idea of *Juche*. They declared that the ultimate objective of the Party is to build socialist and communist society, while its immediate objective is to carry out a people's democratic revolution against U.S. imperialism and fascist rule in south Korea, overthrowing the corrupt colonial and semi-feudal social system and setting up a people's democratic regime on its grave and, further, to fulfil the great cause of reunification of our homeland, the nation's desire and aspiration.

The fighting goal and program put forth by the Revolutionary Party for Reunification reflect the law of socio-economic development and the unanimous aspirations of the people of all walks of life in south Korea. As such, they constitute the joint political program of all the patriotic, democratic forces in south Korea in their fight against the colonial rule of the U.S. imperialist aggressors and for the democratic development of society and the independent, peaceful reunification of our country. They constitute the aim of struggle of the entire south Korean people.

The organizations of the Revolutionary Party for Reunification took an active part in the June 3 Uprising of 1964 against the traitorous "ROK-Japan talks," the August Struggle of 1965 to reject the "ROK-Japan agreements," the struggle against the puppet presidential and puppet national assembly "elections" in 1967 and many other struggles, and are now playing a leading role in the revolutionary struggle of the south Korean people. In the course of struggle the Party has undergone steady revolutionary training and has gained the confidence of the south Korean people and increasing influence among them.

Today the south Korean revolutionaries are consolidating the organizations of the Revolutionary Party for Reunification, firmly rallying the patriotic people around it and are launching a heroic anti-U.S. struggle for national salvation: underground, in the mountains, in the prisons, and even on the gallows.

Comrades, in order to vanquish the counterrevolution and

achieve the victory of the revolution in south Korea, it is necessary to steadily strengthen the revolutionary forces. Only when the forces of the revolution are adequately prepared, can they react in time to repel the enemy's counterrevolutionary offensive and, further, meet the great revolutionary event in full readiness.

What is of paramount importance in preparing the revolutionary forces is to strengthen the Marxist-Leninist Party—the General Staff in the revolution—and rally the workers and peasants closely around it to build a firm central revolutionary force. The south Korean revolutionaries should strive to expand and strengthen Party forces everywhere there are workers, peasants and other revolutionary masses, and root themselves deeply in the masses. To expand and consolidate the mass base of the Party it is necessary to continue to set up mass organizations in various forms among the working people and to solidify them.

All the social groups interested in the revolution must be welded into a single political force at the same time that the main detachment of the revolution is being built up. Only in this way can the counterrevolutionary forces be isolated completely and the overwhelming supremacy of the revolutionary forces be guaranteed. The revolutionary organizations of south Korea should do everything possible to form an anti-U.S. united front for national salvation embracing all patriotic political parties, social organizations, different sectors of the people and individual public figures under the banner of anti-imperialism, anti-fascism and democratization. They should make particularly active efforts to firmly integrate the student youth into the revolutionary ranks and strengthen the organizational ties between them and the workers and peasants who constitute the main force of the revolution.

Only in the course of a widespread mass struggle can the revolutionary forces steadily grow in scope and strength. Only amid the flames of an active revolutionary struggle does the political awakening of the masses become intense; only then is the work of organizing them accelerated; and only then do the activists of the revolution become more numerous and the revolutionary organizations increase their militancy. The more urgent the task of increasing and developing the revolutionary forces in south Korea, the more actively should the mass struggle against the U.S. imperialist aggressors and their lackeys be organized and unfolded, and correct strategic and tactical guidance for it be ensured. What is important here is to analyse and judge the prevailing situation scientifically, taking due account of the requirements of the development of the revolution and the level of consciousness of the masses and, on this basis, put forth suitable fighting slogans and choose the right forms and methods of struggle, skilfully taking advantage of all possibilities, including the inner contradictions and weaknesses of the enemy. The south Korean revolutionaries and people should firmly push the revolutionary movement forward by correctly combining diverse forms and methods of struggle— political and economic struggles, legal, semi-legal and illegal struggles, violent and non-violent struggles, large- and small-scale struggles.

An important task facing the south Korean revolutionaries and patriotic people at the present stage is the positive development of the mass struggle for the democratization of society and against the colonial rule of U.S. imperialism and fascist suppression by its henchmen. It is important to organically link the political struggle against U.S. imperialist colonial rule and fascist military dictatorship and for the attainment of democratic rights—including freedoms of speech, the press, assembly, association and demonstration—with the economic struggle of the toiling masses for the right to exist. The struggle of the student youth for political liberty must be made more purposeful and conscious and their democratic movement must be closely combined with the political struggle of the workers and peasants. Revolutionary forces must be built up so as to crush counter-revolutionary violence by revolutionary violence, always answering violence with violence.

If the south Korean revolutionaries and people build a solid political army through struggle and constantly accumulate their revolutionary forces, they will be ready and able to meet the decisive hour of the revolution. In this way they will eventually topple the present reactionary regime and set up a people's democratic regime, thereby definitely achieving the objectives of the south Korean revolution.

True, the south Korean revolution still has a thorny path ahead, before it achieves victory. But neither the enemy's frenzied endeavors nor any number of trials and tribulations can check its triumphant advance and block the path of the south Korean revolutionaries and patriotic people who have risen in a sacred fight for freedom and liberation, deeply convinced of the justness of their cause.

The people in the southern half are not alone in their revolutionary struggle. They have a powerful revolutionary base in the northern half. Needless to say, the south Korean revolution is a struggle of the south Korean people themselves for their liberation from national and class oppression and exploitation by the U.S. imperialist aggressors and their minions. The oppressed and exploited masses can win freedom and emancipation only through their own revolutionary struggle. Therefore, the south Korean revolution must, in all situations, be made by the south Korean people on their own initiative. But it is the obligation and responsibility of the people in the northern half, as a part of the same nation, to actively support the south Korean people in their revolutionary struggle. The general international situation is now changing to the disadvantage of the counterrevolution and in favor of the revolution. The progressive peoples of all continents denounce U.S. imperialism for its aggressive policy on south Korea and strongly support and encourage the south Korean people in their righteous liberation struggle.

The disintegration of U.S. imperialist colonial rule and the triumph of the revolutionary cause of the people in south Korea are certain.

Comrades, the U.S. imperialist occupation of south Korea has partitioned our territory and split our nation; it has not only visited untold misery and suffering on the south Korean people but brought national calamity to the entire Korean people and set up a great obstacle to the co-ordinated development of Korean society as a whole.

To reunify the divided homeland is the greatest and most pressing national task for the entire Korean people at present. Its solution brooks not a moment's delay.

The whole world knows our Party's policy on national reunification. We have made it clear time and again that if democratic figures with a national conscience come to power in south Korea and demand the withdrawal of U.S. troops, release political prisoners and guarantee democratic freedoms, we are ready to hold negotiations with them any time and any place on the question of the peaceful reunification of the country. Even after the present south Korean rulers staged the fascist military coup and usurped power, we advanced the most fair and reasonable proposals for the reunification of our homeland and made consistent efforts to realize them. We did this in the hope that they would desist from their treacheries to the country and people and would take a truly national stand. More than once we proposed to the south Korean authorities that after the U.S. imperialist aggression army had been driven out of south Korea, the north and the south should each reduce their armies to 100,000 men or less, conclude an agreement to refrain from using armed force against each other, initiate such measures as economic and cultural exchanges and visits of individuals between north and south and establish a unified, democratic government through a free north-south general election. We proposed that such a general election be held when the basic conditions are provided for reunifying the country peacefully in accordance with the free will of the Korean people; if such a general election were not immediately acceptable to them for some reason or other, a Confederation of north and south Korea would be established first as a transitional step for solving urgent matters of common concern for the nation and hastening the reunification of our homeland.

But the south Korean rulers have been dead set against the independent, peaceful reunification of the country, each time ignoring our just proposals which reflect the unanimous aspirations of the whole nation.

The south Korean puppets, under the aegis of the U.S. imperialists and the Japanese militarists, are yelling that the reunification of Korea must be a "reunification by prevailing over communism," and that it is necessary for them to foster their own power for this; they prattle about actions to "protect" south Korea against the fictitious "threat of southward aggression." This is nothing but a smokescreen covering their aggressive design to stifle the south Korean revolution, and invade the northern half of the Republic by force of arms. With such absurd pretexts, the enemy schemes to perpetuate the occupation of south Korea by the U.S. imperialist aggression army on the one hand, and on the other, reinforces the aggressive armed forces on a large scale, expanding military installations and madly stepping up war preparations in south Korea.

The "reunification by prevailing over communism" vociferously advocated by the south Korean rulers means wiping out communism to attain "reunification." This is no more than a fantastic daydream, a feeble-minded babble. For 25 years now, the people in the northern half of the Republic, using communist ideas as their guiding principle, have been building an independent sovereign state, rich and strong, and creating their new, happy life. Communist ideas have taken firm root in the hearts of the people in the north and have been converted into a great indestructible material force. To reunify the country by excluding the Communists in Korea is, in fact, to reject reunification and leave south Korea forever in the hands of U.S. imperialism, as its colony.

As for the so-called "peaceful reunification program," much vaunted of late by the south Korean puppets, it is nothing but a strategic bit of political propaganda filled with lies and deceits from start to finish, devoid of any formula for the settlement of the question of national reunification. The "peaceful reunification program" and all other clamors of this type is aimed at dampening the ever-increasing trend in south Korea towards independent, peaceful reunification, disguising their treachery to the country and nation, and confusing world public opinion, which supports our national reunification program.

How can we discuss the question of the reunification of the country with traitors to the nation who are blocking its independent, peaceful realization; using bayonets to repress the south Korean people's struggle for it; imploring the U.S. to continue its military occupation of south Korea; ushering into south Korea the aggressor forces of Japanese militarism; selling their fellow countrymen to foreign countries as slaves; and forcing young and middle-aged south Koreans into the war of aggression in Viet Nam as cannon fodder for the U.S. imperialists?

The peaceful reunification of our country is utterly unthinkable as long as the U.S. imperialist aggression army and the present puppets remain in south Korea.

To achieve national reunification, it is essential to expel from south Korea the U.S. imperialist aggressors who are its main obstacle and liquidate their colonial rule, overthrow the present fascist military dictatorship and win the victory of the revolution. When a true people's regime is thus established in south Korea, the reunification of our homeland will be achieved easily by the united efforts of the socialist forces in the northern half of the Republic and the patriotic, democratic forces in south Korea.

No amount of frantic manoeuvering by the U.S. imperialists and their minions can break the staunch fighting will of the Korean people to reunify the country. The entire people of north and south Korea will closely unite and vigorously fight the U.S. imperialists and their stooges to frustrate the insidious machinations of the enemy to perpetuate this national split. Thus, we will definitely achieve the reunification of our homeland.

The Revolutionary Peoples Of Asia Will Win In Their Common Struggle Against U.S. Imperialism *(Excerpt)*

Speech at the Pyongyang Mass Meeting Welcoming Samdech Norodom Sihanouk, Head of State of Cambodia and Chairman of the National United Front of Kampuchea, August 6, 1971

Comrades and friends, for the final victory of the Korean revolution we should strengthen and develop our own internal revolutionary force in every way, while at the same time strengthening our solidarity with the international revolutionary forces.

Today the U.S. imperialists are still entrenched in south Korea, refusing to withdraw and are making desperate efforts to make Koreans fight Koreans. The Japanese militarists with the backing of the U.S. imperialists are stepping up their scheme to invade our country again. Under these circumstances we must not slacken vigilance even for a moment. We must continue to direct great efforts to strengthening our defence capacity, as well as stepping up socialist economic construction in order to make the defence of our fatherland impregnable in any emergency.

Holding aloft the banner of the *Juche* idea, under the wise leadership of our Party our people have followed the revolutionary line of independence, self-support and self-defence, and thereby successfully carried out the historic task of socialist industrialization and built up a defence potential strong enough to crush the imperialists any time they attack us.

Encouraged by the successes scored in the northern half of the Republic, the south Korean people are waging a staunch struggle to overthrow the military fascist dictatorship of the U.S. imperialists and their lackeys, shatter the Japanese militarists' scheme to invade our country again and attain freedom, liberation and the reunification of our fatherland. They are dealing heavy blows at the colonial rule of the U.S. imperialists.

Alarmed by a situation which is developing more and more in favor of the revolution as the days go by, the puppet clique of south Korea clings as always to the coattails of the U.S. imperialists and relies all the more on the Japanese militarists in a vain attempt to put off their doom. In an attempt to cover up their treacherous nature and stifle the movement for peaceful reunification, mounting with irresistible force among the south Korean people, they are noisily advertizing their fraudulent "peaceful reunification programme." This stupid ruse, however, can fool no one, nor can it save the south Korean puppet clique from a doom already sealed.

The Government of the Democratic People's Republic of Korea has made consistent efforts to bring about the peaceful reunification of Korea. Again, last April it advanced an 8-point program for independent, peaceful reunification.

This time, too, the U.S. imperialists and the south Korean puppet clique have not replied to our fair and just program for peaceful reunification—a program reflecting the unanimous desire of the entire nation—and are only indulging in empty talk about peaceful reunification. If the south Korean rulers truly want peaceful reunification, to begin with they must not plead for the permanent stationing of U.S. troops but make them withdraw from south Korea. They must stop colluding with the Japanese militarists and stop bringing them into south Korea. They must stop suppressing the political parties, social organizations and democratic personages of south Korea who call for peaceful reunification but enable them to come out for north-south negotiations for the reunification of the country. They must proceed from the stand that the Korean question must be solved by the Koreans themselves.

Apart from the question as to whether or not the south Korean rulers accept our 8-point peaceful reunification program, if they truly want reunification, why are they afraid of contacts and negotiations between the north and the south?

We are ready to establish contact at any time with all political parties, including the Democratic Republican Party, and all social organizations and individual personages in south Korea.

If the south Korean rulers refuse even initial contacts between the north and the south and only give lip service to peaceful reunification, it will stir up more bitter hatred and wrath among the people. They are openly claiming that the question of reunification can only be discussed after 1973 when their "strength is built up" or even in the second half of the 1970's. Their motive is to bring in the revived Japanese militarists into south Korea in full force by that time, and then realize their wild ambition of "reunification by prevailing over communism."

Our people will continue to struggle strenuously to step up socialist construction in the northern half of the Republic, to bring about the south Korean revolution by assisting the south Korean people and to get the question of reunification solved independently by the Korean people themselves on a democratic basis and in a peaceful way.

The Korean people's just struggle to force the U.S. imperialist aggressors to withdraw from south Korea, remove tension in Korea and attain the independent, peaceful reunification of our country, is bound to triumph with the constantly growing support and encouragement of the peace-loving people the world over.

NEW YEAR ADDRESS *(Excerpt)*

January 1, 1972

Comrades, the aspirations of the entire people in north and south Korea for peaceful reunification are growing more than ever today. At Panmunjom representatives of the north and south Korean Red Cross organizations met for the first time in the 26 years after liberation to discuss the important question of alleviating the distress of our fellow countrymen living separated from each other in the north and the south. The entire people in north and south Korea are very glad that such contact between the north and the south has been materialized, though belatedly, and are unanimous in expressing the hope that the talks pave the sure way for pulling down the barriers between the north and the south and materializing the peaceful reunification of the country.

Precisely at this juncture the reactionaries and rulers in south Korea have proclaimed the so-called state of emergency, pleading the non-existent "threat of aggression from the north" as their excuse, and have gone into fascist tyranny against the south Korean people. Those bandists are fabricating all sorts of notorious fascist laws every day, suppressing all the elementary democratic liberties such as of speech, the press, assembly and association and keeping the south Korean society constantly in a

143

state of unrest and fear. A few days ago they rigged up a monstrous fascist law entitled "special law on measures for national security" in face of a strong objection from the opposition parties and the public. Such fascist acts of the south Korean reactionaries against the unanimous aspirations of the whole nation and the trend of the times are aimed primarily at suppressing the ever-growing tendency towards peaceful reunification among the south Korean people and frustrating contacts and negotiations between the north and the south.

Originally, the present puppet rulers in south Korea are the military gangsters who usurped the "power" by force of arms with the backing of the U.S. imperialists in order to hold back the trend towards peaceful reunification which was growing rapidly among the south Korean people following the April 19 Popular Uprising of 1960. After they assumed power as puppets, they put up such ostentatious slogans as "independence," "rehabilitation" and "modernization" in their attempt to deceive the south Korean people, but their true colors were exposed long ago in the eyes of the public. Over the past ten years south Korea has travelled not the way to "independence" but to complete dependence, not the way to "rehabilitation" and "modernization" but to total bankruptcy and ruin.

The south Korean puppet clique have lapsed into a serious political and economic crisis past recovery and this gives them an ever-growing unrest and despair. Though they are trying to find a way out of the blind alley by means of proclaiming the so-called state if emergency and starting a new fascist tyranny, this is no more than the death-bed struggle of the doomed.

The south Korean puppet clique are making noise about the fictitous "threat of aggression from the north" while declaring a "state of emergency," and this is an extremely underhand action to deceive the south Korean people and the world public, and beg their masters for a few more weapons and a few more dollars. The trend of history will never leave unchecked such a cowardly behavior of traitors to the nation. The fraudulent trick of those bandits will hoodwink nobody.

Recently the south Korean puppet clique have developed the habit of clamoring that since we have completed war preparations, we will start invasion soon. True, we are building up our defence power. But it is by no means that we aim to solve the question of national reunification by force of arms. It is to defend the country and nation and safeguard our socialist gains from the aggression of the U.S. imperialists and the Japanese militarists.

Our armed forces are entirely for self-defence.

The power of the proletarian dictatorship will resist by employing force only when the imperialists, reactionary classes and counterrevolutionary elements use force against the revolution. This is the universal principle of Marxism-Leninism and a guide to action for the Government of our Republic. Therefore, it is nothing but absurd, false propaganda when the south Korean puppet clique clamor about the "threat of aggression from the north."

As facts show, no one is fooled now by the mendacious propaganda of the south Korean puppet clique. Rather, their fraudulent propaganda and fascist suppression arouse great indignation and protest among the south Korean people and world people. Even some of the reactionary ruling circles and reptile press in the United States and Japan say that the proclamation of the "state of emergency" in south Korea has not been caused by the threat of southward intrusion but is an invented political trick due to the internal situation, and is an attempt to tide over the social crisis. A Western press reported that the declaration of the "state of emergency" by the south Korean rulers is not due to the "threat of aggression from the north" but to many problems to be solved internally, and that it aims to smother the ever-growing discontent of the south Korean people caused by the acute economic crisis, and suppress the demonstration struggle of the youth and students, the protest of the intellectuals and the resistance of the opposition parties.

The south Korean puppet clique should no longer entertain the foolish hope that the U.S. imperialists and Japanese militarists can deliver them from ruin. The times and circumstances have changed. The days are gone when the U.S. imperialists decided the internal affairs of other countries at their discretion; they have long been on the decline where they cannot escape their doom. The U.S. imperialists are now in a serious political and economic crisis at home and stand in total international isolation. The Sato clique of Japan is also staggering because of the discord within the ruling circles and the strong anti-government struggle of the broad sectors of the popular masses. In the last analysis, there is little difference between the positions of the south Korean puppet clique and those of their masters. Just as they were unable to relieve from ruin the Chiang Kai-shek gang of Taiwan and Thieu band of South Viet Nam, the U.S. imperialists and the Sato clique of Japan will never be able to save the south Korean puppet clique.

Even now when the situation is taking such a turn, the south Korean puppet clique keep clinging to the U.S. imperialists and the Japanese militarists in their efforts to maintain their puppet rule. They are begging U.S. imperialism not to "reduce" its aggressive armed forces in south Korea; the latter, finding itself in a scrape, is paying lip service to "cutback." The Japanese militarist aggressive forces have been called into south Korea again, this time by the puppet clique there. Such traitorous acts of the south Korean puppet clique against the nation only help to hasten their own ruin.

Furthermore, the south Korean puppet clique are dreaming of "reunification by prevailing over communism," with the backing of the U.S. imperialists and the Japanese militarists. This is really a ridiculous nonsense.

History has already furnished an ample proof that nothing can destroy communism. The communist movement has over 100 years of history, counting only from the Paris Commune. All the imperialists and their lackeys have opposed communism, but so far none of them have succeeded in destroying it.

The successive puppet rulers of south Korea, too, without exception, have made every desperate attempt ot oppose communism under the slogan of anti-communism. But communism, far from being destroyed in our country, has rather gained in scope and strength with each passing day. In the northern half of the Republic communist ideology became an absolutely dominant ideology long ago, and has turned into a great material force in all fields of politics, economy, culture and military. Communist ideology has struck deep roots even in the hearts of many south Korean revolutionaries and people. Such being the situation now, it is quite clear that the south Korean puppet clique's dream of "reunification by prevailing over communism" is under no circumstances likely to come true.

The south Korean puppet clique must face the stern reality of today. If they do not renounce the outdated way of thinking that they are following now, but persist in the dirty act of betraying the country and the nation, going against the historical trend, they will not be able to find a way out. If the south Korean rulers want to find some way out, they should not resort to the sordid trickery, as they are doing now, but should honestly admit their crimes, stop their acts of selling out the country and the nation to the U.S. imperialists and Japanese militarists, discontinue their fascist suppression of the south Korean people at once, and respond to the earnest call of the Government of our Republic to realize peaceful reunification through negotiations between the Koreans themselves.

The Government of the Democratic People's Republic of Korea has advanced time and again the most fair and reasonable proposals for the independent, peaceful reunification of the country. Last year alone, the Government of the Republic put forward 8-point proposals for peaceful reunification at the Fifth Session of the Fourth Supreme People's Assembly; particularly in our speech on August 6, we once again clarified our readiness to make contact at any time with all political parties, including the Democratic Republican Party, social organizations and individual personalities in south Korea. All our proposals and suggestions for the independent, peaceful reunification of the country have met with enthusiastic support and response from the broad sectors of the people and personalities from various strata in south Korea, to say nothing of the people in the northern half of the Republic. The south Korean rulers, too, must have the courage to respond to our fair and just proposals, keeping abreast of this nation-wide trend. This will be the only correct act befitting them as Koreans. And only when they do this, I suppose, will the south Korean puppet rulers be able to redeem themselves even in some measure from the crimes they have committed against the country and the people, though a little too late, and find a way out to save themselves.

If the south Korean rulers renounce their reliance on the outside forces and depart from the road of treachery to the nation and return to the position which is truly Korean, we will not ask about their past but will peacefully settle the question of national reunification with them.

In future too, our Party and the Government of the Republic will continue to advocate the independent, peaceful reunification of the country and make every effort for its materialization. But if the south Korean puppet clique do not respond to us in spite of our patient efforts, but keep following the road of betraying the nation, they will ruin themselves, without redeeming their crimes, as traitors forever.

U.S. imperialism is on the decline today, but its aggressive nature remains unchanged and it continues its death-bed struggle. The signboard of "peace" put up by the U.S. imperialists is nothing but a screen to mislead people. Nixon is a rascal, more vicious and crafty than anyone else. The U.S. imperialists do not give up their wild ambition to perpetuate our country's split and make south Korea their permanent colony. They instigate the south Korean puppet clique to continue with aggressive provocations against the northern half of the Republic. And the Japanese militarists, revived by U.S. imperialism, openly reveal their wild design to invade our country again. The Japanese militarists, the "shock force" of U.S. imperialism, are fully prepared to take part in an aggressive war against our country and are watching for a chance of aggression all the time.

Under these conditions all the people in north and south Korea should sharpen their vigilance against the aggressive manoeuvring of the U.S. imperialists and Japanese militarists. Our people can never allow the U.S. imperialists and Japanese militarists to rob them of their country and become slaves for the latter, and repeat the disgraceful history of 1910 when their country was lost. The entire Korean people, irrespective of different political views and religious beliefs, should unite firmly under the banner of the country's defence and independent reunification, and wage an active struggle to frustrate the manoeuvres of the U.S. imperialists and Japanese militarists for aggression.

Even those who committed crimes against the country and the nation in the past should turn out valiantly in a nationwide struggle against the aggression of the U.S. imperialists and Japanese militarists and for the independent reunification of the country, thereby making up for their crimes. If they want to atone for their crimes against the nation, the south Korean rulers should also join in this struggle. They should struggle to drive out the U.S. imperialists, instead of imploring them not to pull out of south Korea, and should not try to usher in the Japanese militarists into south Korea but should fight to smash their manoeuvres for resumption of aggression.

If all the people in the north and the south wage a struggle in firm, monolithic unity, they will be fully able to frustrate the invasion of any imperialists. If the U.S. imperialists and Japanese militarists dare to unleash a war of aggression in our country, the entire north and south Korean people will unite and fight a showdown battle against the enemies, annihilate the aggressors completely and reunify the divided country.

This year the General Association of Korean Residents in Japan (*Chongryon*) organizations and all the Korean nationals in Japan should continue a vigorous struggle to actively protect all the policies of the Workers' Party of Korea and the Government of the Republic, defend their democratic national rights and further advance national education. The Korean nationals in Japan should fight unyieldingly to expedite the peaceful reunification of the homeland. In firm unity with the Japanese people and broad democratic forces of Japan, they should unfold a dynamic struggle against the Japanese militarists' menoeuvres to reinvade south Korea and the hostile policy of the Japanese reactionaries toward the Democratic People's Republic of Korea. In particular, the Korean nationals in Japan should smash up the splitting acts and all the subversive activities of the U.S. and Japanese reactionaries and the factionalists, further consolidate their ranks, rally themselves closely around the *Chongryon* and wage a vigorous struggle.

The international situation is now developing in favor of the revolutionary cause of our people. The anti-imperialist, re-volutionary forces of the world are growing in scope and strength with each passing day; more and more countries actively support and encourage our people in their struggle for independent, peaceful reunification.

Our Party and the Government of the Republic will, this year too, try hard to strengthen their militant solidarity with the revolutionary peoples of the world and promote relations of friendship and co-operation with the peoples of all the countries supporting our people's righteous struggle. In particular, we will unfold a powerful joint struggle against the U.S. and Japanese imperialists and their stooges, in firm unity with the peoples in China, Indo-China, Japan and other Asian countries. By so doing, we will smash up the U.S. imperialists' notorious "Nixon doctrine" and the Japanese militarists' machination for overseas aggression, thus safeguarding peace in Asia and the rest of the world and bringing about a more favorable turn in our people's cause of independent, peaceful reunification.

On Immediate Political and Economic Policies of the Democratic People's Republic of Korea and Some International Problems *(Excerpt)*

Answers to the Questions Raised by
Newsmen of the Japanese Newspaper *Yomiuri Shimbun*,
January 10, 1972

On the Problem of the Reunification of Our Country

Today the general situation of our country is developing very favorably for the struggle of our people for the independent, peaceful reunification of the country.

The successes of socialist construction made in the northern half of the country under the banner of the *Juche* idea further consolidate the political and economic basis for the independent reunification of the country, give great hope and confidence to the people of the southern half and vigorously rouse them to the struggle for the peaceful reunification of the country.

Lately, a tendency towards peaceful reunification is rapidly growing and the struggle against the fascist rule and for the democratization of society is gaining momentum as never before in south Korea. The massive advance of the student youth and people that has continued before and after the "election" of the puppet president held last year, and brisk arguments about national reunification in the public and political circles show that the tendency of opposing the present ruling system and demanding peaceful reunification is rising in south Korea with an irresistible force.

As our policy for the peaceful reunification enjoyed unanimous support not only of the Korean people but of the broad public opinion of the world, and the tendency towards peaceful reunification grew in south Korea, even the south Korean authorities who had rejected any contact between the north and the south could not but come out to the north-south Red Cross talks, pressed by the trend of the times. Though it is rather late and the scope of problems being discussed is limited, the preliminary talks between the north and south Red Cross organizations now being held at Panmunjom are very significant, at any rate since Koreans have got together to discuss internal affairs of the nation. It can be said that this is a step forward in the struggle of our people for reunifying the divided country peacefully.

Our stand on the talks between the north and south Red Cross organizations is clear. We want to mitigate, even a day earlier, the sufferings our people are undergoing owing to the division, by bringing the talks to a success with all our sincerity and pave the way, with it as a stepping stone, to the peaceful reunification of the country.

But the stand of the south Korean authorities is quite opposite. From the first day they were compelled to come out to the talks, they dragged on the talks under this or that pretext and poured cold water upon the growing tendency towards the peaceful reunification, saying: "Don't get too much excited," and "It is premature." Moreover, saying that we would soon "invade the south" because we have already finished war preparations, they proclaimed a "state of national emergency" and are newly trumping up various evil fascist laws to buttress it, and deliberately aggravating the situation.

Such a racket kicked up by the south Korean puppet clique cannot be interpreted otherwise than a design to prolong their remaining days by putting down the ever-growing tendency towards peaceful reunification in south Korea, frustrating contacts and negotiations between the north and the south and perpetuating the split of the country. It is not an accident that even some reactionary ruling circles and government-controlled press in the United States and Japan say that the proclamation of the "state of emergency" in south Korea is not because of the threat of "southward aggression" but, rather, a political trick hatched up because of the internal situation.

With such a foolish trick the south Korean rulers can deceive nobody and solve nothing.

It seems, that frightened by the rapid change of the internal and external situations to their disadvantage, they are going on the rampage. But, they need to cool their heads and think over matters calmly.

Now the times and situation have changed.

The situation today is different from that of the 40's when the U.S. imperialists could divide our country into north and south, abusing the name of the "UN." The day has gone when the U.S. imperialists could meddle in the affairs of other countries and rule the roost.

Now the U.S. imperialists and the Japanese militarists can hardly attend to their own affairs.

We think the time has come when the south Korean rulers should give up the anti-national stand they have held to seek a way out by clinging to the coattails of the U.S. imperialist aggressors and ushering in the Japanese aggressors, turning their back on the compatriots.

If the south Korean rulers are to find a true way out, they should come to the national stand, give up even now their absurd assertion that they would "build up strength" with the backing of outside forces to overpower north Korea by force and attain "reunification by prevailing over communism," and accept our fair and aboveboard proposals to reunify the country in a peaceful way by joining the efforts of the Korean people themselves.

You asked me about our concrete program for the reunification of the country. Our program for national reunification is not different from the previous one. We have invariably maintained that the question of our country's reunification, an internal affair of our nation, should be solved not by the interference of outside forces but by the efforts of the Korean people themselves, not by means of war but in a peaceful way.

We reclarified the program for the independent, peaceful reunification of the country in the 8-point proposals for national salvation advanced at a session of the Supreme People's Assembly of the Democratic People's Republic of Korea held in April last year, in the speech made on August 6 last year and in the New Year Address this year. We will invariably make all our efforts in future to realize the program.

A successful conclusion of the talks now going on between the north and south Red Cross organizations amid the great interest of the whole nation will create a favorable atmosphere for the peaceful reunification of the country.

The south Korean authorities, talking about some sort of "stage," prattle that this can be done and that cannot be done and that only some kind of undertakings must be done first and the other things be deferred. This is a delaying tactic and is not an attitude for solving problems.

If the north-south Red Cross talks yield good results and mutual and free traffic is realized between the families, relatives and friends torn apart in the north and the south, their sufferings will be lessened and, at the same time, the frozen sentiment between north and south will be thawed and mutual understanding deepened in this course.

It is a matter of vital importance for the peaceful reunification of the country, as well as for peace in Asia and the rest of the world, to remove tension in our country.

In order to remove tension in Korea, it is necessary, first of all, to replace the Korean Armistice Agreement with a peace agreement between north and south. We hold that a peace agreement should be concluded between north and south and the armed forces of north and south Korea be cut drastically under the conditions where the U.S. imperialist aggressor troops are withdrawn from south Korea.

We have made it clear more than once that we have no intention to "invade the south." If the south Korean rulers have no intention to "march north for reunification," there will be no

reason for them to refuse to conclude a peace agreement between north and south. If they truly want peace in our country
and peaceful reunification, they should agree to conclude a
peace agreement between north and south, instead of clamoring
about the fictitious "threat of southward aggression."

We advocate strengthening contacts and ties between north
and south and holding north-south political negotiations to
solve the question of national reunification.

Many problems arise in putting an end to the tragedy of national split and reunifying the country peacefully. All these
problems can be satisfactorily solved only through political
negotiations between north and south.

We are ready to have negotiations with all political parties of
south Korea including the Democratic Republican Party, the
New Democratic Party and the Nationalist Party at any time and
at any place agreed upon. Now the south Korean authorities are
talking this or that without having a meeting. It is not an attitude for solving the question of reunification peacefully to reject negotiations, talking about "peaceful reunification" only in
words. In order to solve the question of the reunification of the
country peacefully, various political parties of north and south
Korea are required to hold bilateral or multilateral negotiations
briskly for exchanging political views on national reunification
and finding a reasonable way for peaceful reunification.

We always keep our door opened to anyone for negotiations
and contacts between the north and the south. If anyone,
though he committed crimes against the country and the
people, sincerely repents of his past doings and takes a road of
patriotism for the peaceful reunification of the country, we will
not ask about his crimes but gladly negotiate with him about the
question of the country's reunification.

When all the Koreans unite and fight along the road for the
reunification of the country, we will surely be able to drive out
the U.S. and Japanese aggressors, tide over the crisis of national
ruin created in south Korea, and achieve the peaceful reunification of the country without fail. We are sure that though the
question of Korean reunification is still complicated there is a

prospect of peacefully solving it sooner or later in accordance
with the will of our people and on the principle of national
self-determination.

Talk With Journalists of the
U.S. Newspaper, New York Times

May 26, 1972

I am sure you have seen for yourselves and sensed how the Korean people feel toward the United States here in our country.

They do not have good sentiments toward the United States. Our people have a very strong anti-U.S. feeling. Probably this feeling has offended you Americans.

It is natural that the Korean people should have ill feeling toward the United States. U.S. imperialism is the aggressor which has invaded our country. No people can have warm feelings toward an aggressor who invades their country, can they?

The Korean people's anti-U.S. sentiments grew very strong, particularly because they suffered too much damage at the hands of the U.S. imperialists during the Fatherland Liberation War.

During this war, they suffered tremendous damage because of the U.S. imperialists' barbarous acts of aggression. I do not think there is any Korean who did not sustain a loss in the war. Every Korean suffered a loss in some way or other. If he did not suffer personally, at least his family, relatives, or friends did.

In Pyongyang, for example, the indiscriminate bombing of the U.S. imperialists left few houses intact. The entire city was re-

157

duced to ashes and tens of thousands of people were killed in cold blood. The same was true in Wonsan, Hamhung and other cities. Even our villages were all burned to ashes in the last days of the war.

Having suffered such severe damage at the hands of the U.S. imperialists, the Korean people cannot have good sentiments towards the United States.

Even after the armistice the United States continued an unfriendly attitude towards our country.

The Armistice Agreement stipulated that a political conference of the two sides would be held immediately after the war to settle the Korean question by peaceful means. However, the United States did not abide by this stipulation. As a result, our country is still in a state of ceasefire today. No peace agreement has been concluded and there has been no progress in the work of solving the Korean question peacefully. Therefore, I always tell our people that generations are changing, but the target of our struggle remains the same.

The U.S. authorities have persisted in their aggressive acts against our country in violation of the Armistice Agreement. Even after the *Pueblo* incident, the United States continued its aerial reconnaissance of our country. This places our country in a perpetual de facto state of war.

As this state of war has continued since the ceasefire, we have been forced to step up building our defence and invest heavily in it. Frankly speaking, this enormous expenditure on defence building has, to a certain extent, slowed down the rise in the living standards of the people. Our people also blame the United States for this.

Thus, they have strong anti-U.S. feelings because they suffered great damage at the hands of the U.S. imperialists during the Fatherland Liberation War. Moreover, they have ill feeling toward the United States because the U.S. imperialists have been unfriendly towards our country and continued aggressive acts in violation of the Armistice Agreement even in the postwar period.

The tense situation forces us to continue to step up preparations against war. We make no secret of this. Who can guarantee that the U.S. imperialists will not attack our country again? Neither you nor I, nor anyone else. So we are openly making war preparations in order to defend the country from enemy aggression.

The most important thing in our war preparations is to teach all our people to hate U.S. imperialism. Otherwise, we will not be able to defeat the U.S. imperialists who boast of their technological superiority.

Therefore, we are intensifying ideological education, to imbue the people with hatred for U.S. imperialism. I think this is quite a natural and correct thing for us to do. We do not have to stop the anti-U.S. education we have been giving to our people or conceal the fact that we are educating them in anti-U.S. ideas just because you come to our country, do we?

You must understand our people's ill feeling toward the United States.

You have just said that you hope this abnormal situation between our country and the United States will improve. So do we. We do not want to have many enemies.

Now, let me answer the questions you have raised.

To begin with, I would like to refer to the question of relations between the Democratic People's Republic of Korea and the United States.

You asked me what positive measures should be taken to end the abnormal state of affairs between Korea and the United States. In our opinion this is a very simple matter.

The relations between our country and the United States depend entirely on the attitude of the U.S. government. If the U.S. government changes its policy towards us, we will do the same towards the United States.

If the U.S. government wants to improve its relations with our country, it must, first of all, stop interfering in our internal affairs so that the Koreans can settle the question of Korean reunification independently. It is nearly 20 years now since the Armistice Agreement was signed, so why should U.S. troops continue to occupy south Korea under the guise of "United Nations forces?" Some people say that the U.S. troops are staying on in south Korea to protect it because we might "invade the south." This is a lie. We have declared time and again that we have no intention of invading the south. It is high time to put an end to the situation where U.S. troops play policemen in south Korea under the emblem of "United Nations forces."

The U.S. government disquiets us not only because it has stationed its armed force in south Korea but because it is helping to revive Japanese militarism. We are not happy about the U.S. assistance in the revival of Japanese militarism. We can see from the joint communique of Nixon and Sato of 1969 that the United States is bringing Japanese militarism into south Korea as its agent for aggression against Korea and instigating it to interfere in our country's internal affairs. Following the announcement of the communique, Sato openly declared that he would interfere in Korea's internal affairs. This is another aspect of the unfriendly attitude of the U.S. government toward our country.

On the Korean question in the United Nations, the U.S. government is also taking an unwarranted attitude toward our country. It advocates inviting south Korea to the United Nations unconditionally while attaching conditions to inviting us. It alleges that we do not respect the United Nations Charter, though we have never violated or ignored it. The United States insists that it will allow us to attend the UN General Assembly only if we recognize the unlawful resolutions on the Korean question which were adopted at the United Nations. How can we go to the UN General Assembly under this condition? Furthermore, the United States has been instigating the "United Nations Commission for the Unification and Rehabilitation of Korea" to give annual reports full of lies and fabrications about our country, thus continuing hostile propaganda against us.

Because the U.S. government has invariably pursued such an unfriendly policy toward our country, there has been no improvement in Korea-U.S. relations and the reunification of our country had been greatly hampered.

If the United States wants to improve its relations with our country, it must stop interfering in our internal affairs so that the Koreans can reunify their country by themselves, withdraw its troops disguised as "UN forces" and dissolve the "United

Nations Commission for the Unification and Rehabilitation of Korea." It must not further the partition of the Korean nation but support its reunion. As long as the United States keeps our country divided, our attitude toward the United States will not change. The Korean peninsula is now cut into two parts. If the U.S. troops pull out of south Korea and foreign interference stops, the Koreans will be able to find a common denominator which will enable them to reunify their country by themselves. Furthermore, if the U.S. troops get out of south Korea, I think the Koreans will come to terms easily and our people's anti-U.S. feeling will gradually lessen.

When U.S. President Nixon looked at the Great Wall during his visit to China he said that the barriers dividing nations should be pulled down. If the U.S. government wants to put these words into practice, it must begin with Korea. These days Nixon says he is going to improve relations with China as well as with the Soviet Union. Why, then, should the United States keep its military bases in south Korea? The United States has argued that it keeps them there to prevent communist expansion. Now that it is going to have good relations with the big socialist countries, we consider that there is no excuse for keeping military bases in south Korea. So the United States must quit south Korea at once, dismantling all its military bases and withdrawing its aggressor army.

If the United States wants to better its relations with our country, it must also stop helping to revive Japanese militarism and stop bringing it into south Korea. The United States is trying to substitute Japanese militarism for itself in its invasion of south Korea and reduce south Korea to a commodity market and appendage of Japan. This is an unfriendly, hostile act against our people. The U.S. government must discontinue such unfriendly acts against our country.

If the U.S. government gives up its unfriendly act against our country and stops obstructing our reunification, then there will be no reason why we should be antagonistic to the United States. So we say that the relations between the Democratic People's Republic of Korea and the United States depend not on us, but entirely on the attitude of the U.S. government. We will closely watch the policy the United States adopts toward our country in the future.

The U.S. government should improve relations not only with big countries, but with small countries as well. We do not think improved U.S. relations with big countries will greatly influence its relations with small countries. In fact, the U.S. government has not yet changed its attitude in its relations with small countries.

In the joint communique of the People's Republic of China and the United States, the latter declared that it supports the relaxation of tension on the Korean peninsula and contact between north and south Korea. As for what influence the United States will exert on south Korea in this respect, we must wait and see. If the United States does not support the relaxation of tension in Korea and north-south contact in the future, it will mean that it uttered empty words under pressure.

Our people remember what Nixon said in China. What interests me most is that he said that no barriers should divide the people of the world. We are watching how he is going to put his words into practice.

You asked me if moves such as an exchange of journalists and cultural interchange to promote mutual understanding and reduce tension were possible between the two countries even before the U.S. troops are withdrawn from south Korea. I will answer this briefly.

Frankly, we cannot understand what interests Americans to come to our country. We do not think our people would bring back anything interesting if they visited the United States in the present situation.

We do not mean that we want to shut the door to relations with the United States. But we consider that as long as the fundamental problem between the two countries remains unsolved, an exchange of journalists or cultural interchange would be of little significance.

I am told you feel uncomfortable in our country. If other Americans come here they will return with the same uncomfortable feeling.

We are now intensifying anti-U.S. education among our younger generation so that they will not forget their enemy. As long as the U.S. government's hostile policy toward our country remains unchanged, our policy toward the United States will not change either. Therefore, Americans will not get good impressions here until the fundamental problem between the two countries is solved. If many Americans come to our country in the future, and go back with uncomfortable feelings, we think such visits will not be beneficial.

If the U.S. government discards its hostile policy toward our country, our anti-U.S. feelings may be lessened. Only then will visits and interchange between the two countries be fruitful and interesting to both sides.

Since the U.S. government does not alter its hostile policy toward our country, mutual visits had better be limited in scope, as at present. We do not think that there is no need at all for our journalists to visit the United States. In our opinion, it is necessary for them to go there in order to let the American people hear our true voice, because at present you only hear the voice of the south Korean rulers. We welcome visits by American journalists and democratic figures on a limited scale. Such visits and interchange will help promote understanding between the two peoples.

In the light of our experience in receiving you now, I think it would be a good idea for us to explain to future American visitors how we are conducting anti-U.S. education among our people before they start going on visits.

Next I want to refer to a few points concerning Korea's reunification.

You asked me whether it would be possible to deal with the Korean question in the same way as the Viet Nam question was dealt with at the Geneva Conference in 1954. We think we need not deal with the Korean question in such a way.

The Korean question must be solved by the Koreans themselves on the principle of national self-determination without any foreign interference. Only then can the reunification of our country be achieved peacefully.

The Soviet Union and China actively support this program for national reunification. The Soviet and Chinese governments have issued statements on many occasions supporting our country's program for peaceful reunification.

A prerequisite for the independent settlement of the question of Korean reunification without foreign interference is that the U.S. troops must be withdrawn from south Korea. No war will break out in Korea after they are withdrawn.

When the U.S. troops pull out of south Korea and the people of north and south Korea are united, we can reunify Korea quickly and frustrate the Japanese militarists' manoeuvres to invade Korea again. The Korean people can achieve national unity by their own efforts.

As you know, we are now having contacts with south Korea through the preliminary talks between the north and south Korean Red Cross organizations. Of course, as for the prospects and the results of the talks, we will have to wait and see. But we think that if we Koreans sit down at a conference table, we can find ways for removing the distrust and misunderstanding between the north and the south and attaining national unity.

The north and south Koreans are cold to each other, and distrust and misunderstand each other in many respects because they have had no opportunity to sit down together in one place.

We think distrust and misunderstanding exist between the north and south Koreans on a number of questions.

We believe that the south Korean rulers may invade the northern half of the Republic with the support of the United States and the Japanese militarist forces. The south Korean rulers labor under the misunderstanding that we might attack south Korea. They are also raising "anti-communist" clamors, asserting that we are trying to "communize" south Korea. Due to such distrust and misunderstanding, no progress has yet been made on the question of Korean reunification.

We believe that if we Koreans sit down together, we will be able to remove distrust and misunderstanding and find common denominators and, on this basis, achieve national unity.

These days the south Korean rulers are clamoring for the independent reunification of the country, advocating, though in words only, "self-help," "self-reliance," "self-defence." If we interpret this favorably, we can see some similarity with the idea of independence, self-reliance and self-defence which we advocate.

If we find and develop these common denominators one by one, it will be possible to reach an agreement on achieving national unity.

The difference in social systems in the north and the south must not be made an obstacle to the promotion of national unity and the attainment of reunification.

At present, some foreign journalists say there are two opposite poles in Korea—north Korea's communist system and south Korea's capitalist system—and these two poles cannot be integrated. Once these two poles touch, they say, war will break out again in Korea.

We do not regard south Korea as a capitalist society in the true sense of the word. There are no big monopoly capitalists in south Korea, only a few comprador capitalists. Of course, we are against comprador capitalists. We oppose them because they obstruct the development of the national economy. But we are not against national capitalists and small and medium entrepreneurs. We can say that south Korean society is no more than a society which is just starting to take the road of capitalism, or is inclined to capitalism, or is being influenced by capitalism, or believes in capitalism, or something like that. This does not mean that there is no difference in the social systems in the north and the south.

It is true that there are now differences in ideas and beliefs between the north and the south. But we think we must transcend these differences for the sake of national unity. We have no intention of imposing our socialist system on south Korea. Unless its present rulers try to force us to replace our socialist system with another, there is no reason why we cannot achieve national unity.

If the north and the south establish the principle of each not imposing its social system on the other, then there is no need to fight each other with arms. If neither side is forced to give up its political beliefs, is there any reason for the people of one and the same nation to fight?

It is possible that a country may have different political systems and that people with different beliefs may live together in one country. What political system should be established in south Korea is a matter for the south Korean people themselves to decide. So we consider that even after the country is reunified the present social systems in the north and the south may continue as they are, and the people who have different beliefs may live together in Korea. What is needed here is mutual trust and respect.

We always maintain that our homeland should be reunified independently and peacefully without foreign interference. Furthermore, we hold that the unity of the entire nation should be achieved under conditions in which both sides trust and respect each other, despite the different social systems in the north and the south.

In a speech on August 6 last year, we pointed out that we were ready to have contacts even with the Democratic Republican Party, the ruling party of south Korea. This stems from our desire to create mutual respect.

If the north and the south join hands and make tireless efforts, we will be able to eliminate mutual misunderstanding and distrust gradually, and achieve the reunification of the country independently on a democratic basis. Our country cannot be reunified if outside forces meddle in the Korean question. Foreigners cannot rid our nation of distrust and misunderstanding. That is why we oppose interference of any outside force in the Korean question.

We believe that if there is no outside interference in the Korean question and foreign countries give up obstructionist machinations, the reunification of Korea will definitely be attained the way we are advocating, though it may take time.

You said you want to know what practical measures we are taking to bring about the independent, peaceful reunification of the country. I will outline them briefly.

We are calling for mail exchange and mutual visits and trade and economic co-operation as well between the north and the south.

As for mutual visits of personages we think it also desirable for our deputies to the Supreme People's Assembly and the "national assemblymen" of south Korea to visit each other. If "national assemblymen" of south Korea come to the northern half of the Republic and our deputies to the Supreme People's Assembly go to south Korea and if they sit down at one table and exchange views openheartedly through such mutual visits, it will be a good thing for the reunification of our homeland. It is by no means a bad thing. We want contacts not only with south Korean "national assemblymen" but also with a broad spectrum of political and public figures in south Korea. In other words, we hold that all the political parties and social organizations of north and south Korea should get together in a political consultative conference and exchange wide-ranging views on the question of national reunification.

Furthermore, we have proposed that, if it is impossible to reunify the country at once, a confederation be set up. This means forming a supreme national council with representatives of the north and south Korean governments, mainly for consulting and co-ordinating on matters concerning the national interests of Korea, while maintaining the present different political systems in north and south Korea as they are for the time being.

We have also more than once proposed economic intercourse between the north and the south, proceeding from the immediate interests of the nation. If economic co-operation materializes and we give south Korea what we have in sufficiency and receive what it has in plenty, the economy of both parts will develop more rapidly.

We have also proposed cultural and scientific exchanges between the north and the south.

In addition, we maintain that a peace agreement should be concluded between the north and the south, stipulating that each side refrains from the use of arms against the other and that the numerical strength of the armed forces of the two sides be reduced after the withdrawal of all foreign troops from south Korea. The present arms race between the north and the south is having a considerable effect on the living standards of the people.

We are doing all we can to remove the tension and bring about contact and exchange between the north and the south. True, if mutual visits are made, capitalist influence may be brought into the northern half of the Republic. But we are not in the least afraid of this. We keep our door open so that south Koreans can visit the northern half of the Republic at any time. It is not we but the south Korean rulers who are keeping the door closed. Everything will be settled easily once the south Korean authorities open their door.

But the south Korean rulers are very much afraid to do this. Having declared a "state of emergency" under the pretext of a fictitious "threat of aggression from the north," they are playing all sorts of tricks while the preliminary talks are going on between the north and south Korean Red Cross organizations. They are ruthlessly suppressing those south Koreans who desire reunification. They are even prohibiting "national assemblymen" of the Democratic Republican Party from talking with their New Democratic Party colleagues in the puppet national assembly. The south Korean rulers are now raising an "anticommunist" clamor, holding "anti-communist rallies" and "meetings for the annihilation of communism and against espionage activities" in all parts of south Korea.

We have no intention of invading south Korea, nor do we want to impose our socialist system on south Korea. Nevertheless, the south Korean rulers have declared a "state of emergency" under the pretext of a "threat of aggression from the north" and are intensifying their fascist repression of the south Korean people and clamoring for "reunification through the annihilation of communism." This is not an attitude helpful to national reunification. Their hullabaloo is designed not to bring about a close relationship between the north and the south but to estrange them further. It is intended to prevent the country from being reunified. By "reunification through the annihilation of communism," the south Korean rulers mean to achieve reunification after wiping out the Communists in Korea. In the final analysis, this means that they oppose reunification and want to perpetuate the partition. We do not know who is the author of this racket in south Korea. But we think it betrays their weakness.

We will continue our patient efforts to bring about contacts and dialogue between the north and the south.

We are at present gravely concerned about south Korea's economic subjection to Japan. If the south Korean rulers keep the door between the north and the south closed, Japanese capital will penetrate south Korea, and the latter will become completely subjected to Japan economically.

We do not forget the history of the Japanese imperialists' invasion of our country. They began worming their way into Korea in 1894 under the pretext of protecting Japanese residents in Korea. From then on our country began falling into the status of a Japanese colony.

Japanese militarism revived under the wing of U.S. imperialism is now scheming to invade Korea again. We read an article in the Japanese magazine *World Weekly* which quoted Japanese militarist leaders as saying that Korea should not be reunified for at least a quarter of a century. This shows that the Japanese militarists are watching for a chance to invade Korea again.

We have to heighten our vigilance against the Japanese militarists. We are fully informing all our people, and especially the younger generation, on the history of Japanese militarist aggression in our country so that they will not forget it but keep sharp vigilance against Japanese militarism.

Our country has not yet been reunified, but remains divided into north and south because of the reactionary manoeuvres of the south Korean rulers and the obstructionist activities of outside forces.

Therefore, we think that all the north and south Korean people must unite firmly and struggle actively against the outside forces that hamper the reunification of our country.

You asked me about the relations between our country and Japan. I will touch on this briefly now.

The improvement of relations between our country and Japan depends on the attitude the Japanese government takes.

Good-neighbour relations have not been established up to this date solely because the Japanese government has followed a hostile policy toward our country. The successive cabinets of the Japanese government, from Yoshida to Sato, including those of Kishi and Ikeda, have adopted an unfriendly attitude and a hostile policy toward our country.

If the Japanese government gives up its hostile policy toward our country and wants to establish friendly relations with us, we are fully ready to respond.

However, as long as the Japanese government pursues a hostile policy and takes an unfriendly attitude toward our country, we do not want to improve relations between the two countries by resorting to sycophant diplomacy. The smaller a country is, the greater self-respect its people must have. If the peoples of small countries do not even have self-respect, they cannot survive. We do not want to go to Heaven by turning our right cheek after we have been hit on the left. We have no thought of throwing our self-respect away.

You asked me what is the best gift I could give to our people. It is the reunification of the country.

The Korean people are one people of the same blood. But they are divided because their country is not yet reunified. This is our greatest grief.

At present, because of an artificial barrier in our country many people live separated from their families and relatives for a long time, unable to meet each other, write letters or hear about each other's fate, alive or dead. The artificial barrier which causes this tragic state of affairs must be pulled down as soon as possible and our homeland reunified without fail.

Once our country is reunified, our people will lead as good a life as others, and will live peacefully with the different peoples of the world according to the principles of equality and mutual respect.

From ancient times, the Korean people have been industrious and resourceful. Our people went through suffering and were long subjected to national humiliation, oppression and exploitation, and to aggression by foreign invaders. So, if our people in north and south Korea join efforts and strive to build a new society, we will be able to live as well as others and our country will become a rich, powerful, independent and sovereign state.

Our country has a fairly large population and abundant natural resources. We have trained a large number of competent cadres of our own. Immediately after liberation we had few able technicians. The Japanese imperialists would not pass technology on to the Koreans and even prevented them from learning it. They were so adamant about preventing Koreans from acquiring technical knowledge that before liberation there were only four Korean locomotive drivers. They allowed only Japanese to be locomotive drivers and at best, let Koreans be stokers. In order not to repeat this bitter experience, we devoted great efforts after liberation to training our own cadres. As a result, we have half a million technicians and specialists today. On the basis of the successes already achieved in training cadres, we are planning to increase their number to one million during the Six-Year Plan.

As you see, we have a big population, rich natural resources and a huge army of technicians. So when the country is reunified, we can build a rich and strong country and guarantee our people affluence in a short time.

I will give a brief answer to your question on what was the most difficult of our struggles.

We have had so many difficult struggles that I cannot tell you about them all here and now.

To my mind, one of the most difficult was the struggle to rise up out of the debris after the war.

In the three-year war, every town and village was razed to the ground and every industrial enterprise reduced to ashes. When the war ended, we had to build towns, villages and factories on the ruins where nothing was left and rapidly stabilize the people's living conditions. But we were able to overcome these difficulties and trials and win a great victory in economic construction because we were firmly united with the masses of the people.

We have basically overcome the difficulties in socialist construction. Now the lives of our people are stable. It is true that their living standards are not yet very high. But no one in our country is hungry or in rags or wandering about without a job. Our people all work, receive free education and free medical care. This is a great victory won by our people in socialist construction.

We have laid the basis for rapidly developing the national economy and raising the people's living standards in the future.

As I have already mentioned, we have a huge army of competent cadres, we have built the foundations of a powerful heavy industry centered around the engineering industry and constructed a large number of modern light industrial factories. In particular, we have developed a strong, independent industry which is supplied by our own raw materials. We have laid the basis for the further development of stockbreeding.

All this firmly guarantees the more rapid development of our economy and a bigger rise in the people's standard of living.

Thank you for your attention. Now let me conclude my answers to your questions.

We oppose the reactionary policies of the U.S. government but we do not oppose the American people. We want to have many good friends in the United States.

On Some Problems of Our Party's Juche Idea and the Government of the Republic's Internal and External Policies

Answers to the Questions Raised by Journalists of the Japanese Newspaper Mainichi Shimbun, September 17, 1972

I warmly welcome your visit to our country.

I have received your questionaire through the Central Committee of the Journalists' Union of Korea.

Now, I would like to give brief answers to your questions.

1. Some Problems Involved in the Idea of Juche

You requested me to tell how the *Juche* idea originated.

In a nutshell, the idea of *Juche* means that the masters of the revolution and the work of construction are the masses of the people and that they are also the motive force of the revolution and the work of construction. In other words, one is responsible for one's own destiny and one has also the capacity for hewing out one's own destiny.

We are not the author of this idea. Every Marxist-Leninist has this idea. I have just laid a special emphasis on this idea.

How keenly the necessity of establishing *Juche* is felt and how

173

much emphasis is laid on it may depend on people and on the social and historical backgrounds of a country.

In the course of my struggle for the freedom and independence of our country I came to a firm conviction that we must and could work out our own destiny with our own efforts. Our struggle was hard and complex. We had to solve everything by ourselves and use our own heads to formulate the lines and methods of struggle as well.

Naturally, therefore, we met indescribable difficulties and had to pass through harsh trials. Through this, however, we obtained absolutely unique experience and lessons. We realized that the simple and ordinary working masses, if only they were brought to revolutionary awareness, could display a really great force and carry out the revolution by their own efforts in any adverse and arduous conditions.

Our situation was also extremely difficult right after liberation. We had had no experience of running the state or managing the economy. Our country was very backward, and it was divided into north and south. We could look nowhere for a ready-made solution to the problem of building a new country in this complex situation.

The first problem that confronted us was whether to take the road to capitalism or the road to socialism, so that we might quickly free ourselves from our wretched situation.

The road to capitalism meant preserving exploitation and oppression. This would not only prevent us from rousing the broad masses of the proletariat to the building of a new country, but would also involve the great danger of our country being again subordinated by another imperialist power. It was evident, therefore, that we could not follow the road to capitalism.

However, we could not take the road to socialism immediately. Socialism was what we needed. Subjective desire alone could not obtain it. We were faced with the immediate tasks of the democratic revolution which must be solved before going over to socialism. So we could not just imitate the socialist system.

From the outset we had to use our own brains to determine a political system that would serve the interests of the working class and other sectors of the working masses and that would be able to rally the broad masses of people. We also had to determine the way to effect democratic social reforms that might suit the specific conditions of our cuntry. Accordingly, for agrarian reform, we went to farm villages and stayed many days with the peasants, exploring ways and means that would suit our rural situation.

Our experience showed that endeavoring to solve our problems in this way to suit our actual conditions was much better than mechanically copying foreign ways. Our post-liberation struggle for the building of a new country validated our *Juche* idea and increased our faith in it.

Then, we waged the harsh three-year war against the U.S. imperialists, and our country was reduced to ashes. This rendered our task of building socialism even more difficult.

The U.S. imperialists destroyed not only the dwelling houses and property of our workers and peasants but also the economy of the small and medium entrepreneurs and the rich peasants as well. During their socialist revolutions, other nations eliminated the capitalist and rich peasant classes by expropriating them, but we had no need to do so. Immediately after liberation we consistently pursued the policy of encouraging the economy of the small and medium entrepreneurs, who could fight side by side with the workers and the peasants against imperialism. Moreover, it was necessary for us to protect national capital as at that stage our industry was not fully developed. However, since the economy of the small and medium capitalists and the rich peasants was utterly destroyed by the war, our Government had no need to take the trouble of reviving it.

Now that everything had been ravaged by the war, there was little difference between the small and medium entrepreneurs and the urban craftsmen. Everyone became a proletarian, so to speak. They had to pool their efforts and go along the road to socialism, this was the only way for them to subsist. In order to shore up their completely devastated agriculture, the peasants, too, had to do the same.

Proceeding from the Marxist-Leninist proposition that co-operation, even when it is based on primitive techniques, is far superior to private farming, and considering the actual fact that our peasants badly needed to work together to free themselves from their plight, we adopted an original method—boldly pushing ahead with the socialist transformation of agriculture before industrialization. As regards the small and medium entrepreneurs and rich peasants we also chose a unique way—drawing them into the co-operatives and remoulding them on socialist lines because there was no necessity to expropriate them.

Again experience justified our Party's line of solving all problems in the interest of our people and in conformity with the specific conditions of our country without recourse to any ready-made formula or proposition.

Through this course we have been more deeply convinced that the correct stand and attitude to maintain in revolution and construction is to settle all problems in the interest of our people and in conformity with the specific conditions of our country, believing in and relying on our own strength, with the consciousness of masters of the revolution.

Our revolution has traversed and is traversing a very complicated and difficult road. Whenever we were confronted with difficulties and ordeals, we maintained the attitude of a master towards the revolution and thereby achieved glorious victories. This process made our conviction still more unshakable—a conviction that only by firmly relying on the *Juche* idea can one thoroughly adhere to the revolutionary stand of the working class and creatively apply Marxism-Leninism to the realities of one's country.

You asked me whether you may understand that the *Juche* idea is embodied as independence in politics, self-reliance in the economy and self-defence in national defence. Your understanding is quite correct.

Establishing *Juche* means taking the attitude of a master towards the revolution and construction. Since the masters of the revolution and construction are the masses of the people, they should take a responsible attitude of a master towards the revolution and construction. The attitude of a master finds expression in an independent and creative stand.

Revolution and construction are a work for the masses of the people, a work that has to be carried out by them alone. Therefore, the transformation of nature and society demands their independent position and creative activity.

Based on the interests of our people and on the interests of our revolution, our Party has always maintained a firm independent stand in mapping out all policies and lines through its own efforts and responsibly carrying out the revolution and construction on the principle of self-reliance. Our Party has always been able to win victories because it believed in the strength of the people and gave full play to their revolutionary zeal and creative activity, thus encouraging them to realize themselves all potentialities and reserves, and solve all problems arising in the revolution and construction to suit our true realities.

Adhering to the stand of master in the revolution and construction and enhancing the role as master are integrated concepts with different aspects. You may say that the independent stand is concerned with defence of the rights of the master and discharging the responsibility as such, whereas the creative stand concerns the development of the role of the people, the masters, in remaking nature and reconstructing society. In other words, the independent stand is the fundamental stand which we must maintain in the revolution and construction, and the creative stand is the fundamental method that we must apply in transforming nature and society.

To adhere to the independent stand it is most important that we fully guarantee independence in politics.

Independence is what keeps man alive. If he loses independence in society, he cannot be called a man; he differs little from an animal. We might say that socio-political life is more valuable to a man than physical life. He is a social being. If he is forsaken by society and deprived of political independence, though he seems alive, he is virtually dead as social human being. That is why the revolutionaries deem it far more honorable to die in the fight for freedom than to keep themselves alive in slavery.

Ignoring independence is tantamount to ignoring man himself. Who likes to live shackled to others? Why did people fight to overthrow the feudal system in former days and why are the working class fighting against the capitalist system today? Needless to say, working people wanted to extricate themselves from feudal slavery just as they want to free themselves from capitalist exploitation and oppression. We are fighting against imperialism in order to liberate our nation completely from its yoke and enable it to enjoy freedom as a sovereign nation. In a word, all the revolutionary struggles aim to attain freedom from either class or national subjugation; they are struggles of the people in defence of their independence. Our struggle for the building of socialism and communism, too, is, in the long run, to enable the people to extricate themselves from many forms of subjugation and lead independent and creative lives as masters of nature and society.

In order to become the master of its own destiny, a nation must have an independent government and firmly guarantee political independence. This is why the *Juche* idea should first be embodied as the principle of independence in politics.

To guarantee solid independence in politics, there must be a special guiding idea and a capacity for formulating all policies and lines solely in the interests of one's country, according to one's own judgment. The government that acts under pressure from, or instructions of, others cannot be called a genuine people's government responsible for the destiny of the people. A country with this sort of government cannot be regarded as an independent, sovereign state.

The principle of independence in politics demands complete equality and mutual respect among all nations. It opposes both subjugating others and being subjugated by others. A nation that subjugates others can never be free itself.

In strengthening the independence of the country, it is essential to strengthen self-reliance in the economy along with political independence. Without self-reliance in the economy, it is impossible to meet the people's growing material demands, and materially guarantee them a real role as master of the state and society. Economic dependence on others cannot guarantee political independence and without independent economic power, it is impossible to carry through the line of self-defence in national defence.

Self-defence and self-protection are intrinsic to the nature of man. A country must also have the means to defend itself. The line of self-defence in national defence is an essential requirement of an independent and sovereign state. While there are still imperialist aggressors, the state that has no defence power of its own to protect its sovereignty against the internal and external enemies is, in fact, not a fully independent and sovereign state.

Our Party's consistent line of independence in politics, self-reliance in the economy and self-defence in national defence has long since been proved correct and vital by our people through their revolutionary practices.

Next, I am going to say a few words about your question as to what we stress as an embodiment of the *Juche* idea in our present domestic policy.

Embodying the *Juche* idea means powerfully stepping up revolution and construction from an independent and creative stand.

The most urgent problem facing us at present in embodying the *Juche* idea in the Korean revolution is that of bringing about the independent, peaceful reunification of our country.

Our people have been fighting for a long time to rid themselves of the yoke of imperialism, but our national sovereignty is still being trampled underfoot by foreign aggressors in one half of our territory. Nothing is more urgent for our people today than driving out foreign aggressors and establishing national sovereignty throughout our country.

The south Korean rulers have been hampering the independent, peaceful reunification of the country for nearly 30 years, pursuing the policy of dependence on outside forces. Dependence on outside forces is the road to national ruin. This is a serious lesson our people have drawn for themselves from a long history of national suffering. It is also a reality we are now clearly perceiving through the misfortunes and pains of the south Korean people under the U.S. imperialist occupation. Our immediate task is to see that all the people in north and south Korea fight against outside forces in the spirit of independence and self-reliance and rise in the forceful struggle for the independent, peaceful reunification of the country. Achieving this reunification is the most important work in embodying the *Juche* idea in the Korean revolution today.

The central task before us now, to implement the *Juche* idea in the northern half of the Republic, is to free our people from tough labor by dynamically pushing ahead with the three major tasks of the technical revolution.

Our people freed from exploitation and oppression, have now the important task of emancipating themselves from arduous work.

Labor holds the most important place in people's social life. Eliminating fundamental distinctions that exist in work conditions and freeing the people from tough labor will be of great significance in making their lives more independent and creative.

In order to emancipate the people from backbreaking labor, it is imperative to push ahead with the three major tasks of the technical revolution. The three tasks we propose are designed to narrow down the distinctions between light and heavy labor, and between agricultural and industrial work, and to free our women from the heavy burdens of household chores by fully developing techniques by our own efforts. When they are carried out completely, arduous labor in town and country will be largely removed and the class difference in work between the working class and the peasantry be eliminated.

We proposed the three major tasks of the technical revolution as our goal in emancipating our people from arduous labor; we did this instead of merely referring in general terms to the development of heavy industry or light industry. This clearly testifies to our Party's consistent standpoint that economic construction or technical revolution should not be designed for its own sake but should serve as the means to provide the people with fruitful lives as the masters of the state and society. Attaching the greatest importance to people in every respect and serving them—this is precisely the requirement of the *Juche* idea.

Next, you asked me to tell about the education of our youth and children based on the *Juche* idea.

We are greatly concerned with the education of youth and children. This is because they are the reserves of our revolution who must carry forward the revolution through coming generations. Moreover, there is no more important job than that of educating and training people for the progress of society.

It is true that with no material means people can neither live nor develop. In this sense, the economy constitutes the material foundation of social life. However, this is always planned for the benefit of people and would be meaningless without them. It is also the people who create the means of living and improve living conditions. Therefore, what is most important in the development of society is training people to be more dynamic. In order to powerfully push ahead with the revolution and construction, top priority should be given to the work with men, that is, to the work of remoulding men.

The basis of the *Juche* idea is that man is the master of all things and the decisive factor in everything. Remaking nature and society is also for people and it is work done by them. Man is the most precious treasure in the world and he is also the most powerful. All our work is for the people and its success depends on the way we work with them. Education is an important aspect of the work with men.

Education involves training people to be social beings, fully prepared mentally, morally and physically. In order to become social beings, they should first have sound social consciousness. If the younger generation, who were born in this revolutionary era, are not armed with revolutionary ideas and if they are ignorant of science, technique or literature and art as the men in our era of socialist construction, they cannot be called social beings.

Only when people have ideological and cultural background which they should possess as social beings, can they participate as masters in all aspects of social life and energetically accelerate the revolution and construction. This is why our Party always places greater emphasis on education than on any other work.

We regard as the core of education the implementation of the socialist pedagogical doctrine. Its basic principle lies in training people to be reliable revolutionary workers equipped with the ideology, knowledge and a strong physique that will enable them to take the role of master in the revolution and construction.

It is most important in training and educating people to remould their ideology in a revolutionary way. All human actity is determined by ideology. If a man is ideologically backward and morally degenerate, despite his excellent health, he cannot but be regarded as utterly useless and mentally disabled in our society. Therefore, our Party always directs its primary attention to remoulding people's ideology in a revolutionary manner.

In the education of youth and children, we should give top priority to the work of training them in revolutionary ideas. If they hate work and do not serve the state and society, their knowledge and skills will be of no use, however excellent they may be. They must be so equipped with socialist patriotism and a revolutionary world outlook as to work for their people and homeland instead of trying to get promoted or earn money; we should see to it that whatever they learn is useful and that all children and young people grow up into a new type of men with communist moral traits, who are eager to work, protect and take good care of state and social property, and take the lead in the revolution and construction. This is the fundamental requirement of socialist pedagogy.

Today we are making great efforts to enforce universal ten-year compulsory senior-middle-school education. When this has been effected, our rising generation will grow up as an able builder of socialism, equipped with the essentials of a revolutionary world outlook, with a basic knowledge of nature and society, and more than one technical skill. This is of tremendous significance in revolutionizing and working-classizing the entire society, and advancing our socialist construction.

You requested me to give a detailed explanation of the *Juche* idea. But there is no end to it. All the policies and lines of our Party emanate from the *Juche* idea and they embody this idea. The *Juche* idea is not a theory for theory's sake; it is the guiding idea of the revolution and construction in our country that we put forth on the basis of the experiences and lessons obtained through our complicated revolutionary struggles. In our country the *Juche* idea is a stern fact of history established in all aspects of social life. To have a deep understanding of the *Juche* idea, it is necessary to make a detailed study of our Party's policy and our country's reality.

2. On the Foreign Policy of the Government of the Republic

You asked me what influence our foreign policy, based as it is on the *Juche* idea, has in strengthening the solidarity of the socialist countries, in the anti-imperialist struggle and in the consolidation of international democratic forces. I am going to make a few remarks on this question.

As you correctly pointed out, the Government of the Republic formulates its foreign policy on the basis of the *Juche* idea and is guided by this idea in carrying out all its external activities. In a word, our Republic firmly maintains independence in its foreign activities.

The Government of the Republic's independent foreign policy reflects the lofty aspirations of our people and the world's people. In our foreign activity we maintain the principle of increasing internationalist solidarity and co-operation, while holding fast to independence; we are promoting our friendly and cooperative relations with those countries which are friendly toward our country, be they large or small. Neither do we infringe upon the interests of other countries nor do we allow anyone to encroach upon our nation's rights and dignity, or meddle in our country's internal affairs. This foreign policy pursued by the Government of our Republic not only conforms with the interests of the revolution and construction in our country, but it is also in full accord with the interests of world revolution.

The principle of independence held by the Government of our Republic in its external activity is in no way contradicted by proletarian internationalism. There can be no internationalism without independence, and vice versa.

First of all, our Government's foreign policy based on the *Juche* idea is actively contributing to strengthening the solidarity of socialist countries.

The Government of the Republic strictly abides by the principle of independence in its relations with the socialist countries. With the principle of equality and independence we are developing our relations of friendship and co-operation with the socialist countries. And against all hues of opportunism arising within the international working-class movement, too, we are waging our struggle in conformity with the actual conditions of our country, always on the basis of our independent judgment and conviction.

We adhere to our principle based on independence particularly in our efforts to achieve unity and cohesion among the socialist countries. We maintain that all socialist countries should, first, oppose imperialism; second, support the national-liberation movement in colonies and the international working-class movement; third, go on towards socialism and communism; and fourth, attain unity on the principles of non-interference in each other's internal affairs, mutual respect, equality and reciprocity. Although there exist differences of opinion among the fraternal parties and socialist countries, we continue to promote unity and wage a joint struggle in accordance with these four principles.

As for the anti-imperialist struggle, the government of our Republic is fighting in accordance with our own beliefs and our actual situation. Internally, we define as a major revolutionary task the struggle against U.S. imperialism, the sworn enemy of our people, and in our external activities as well, we are actively battling to check and frustrate the U.S. imperialist policies of aggression and war and to defend world peace and security. Our Government regards it as its iron rule to give active support and encouragement to the struggle of the world's people against U.S. imperialism and is endeavoring to increase our solidarity with all the anti-imperialist forces.

With regard to the international democratic movement, the Government of our Republic also adheres to the principle of independence and non-interference. We are doing all we can to support and encourage the revolutionary struggle and democratic movement of the people in the world for peace and democracy, national independence and social progress. We have no intention to interfere or impose our ideas upon them.

Our Government also strives to unite with the new indepencent countries, and all other countries, on the five principles—respect for territorial integrity and sovereignty, non-aggression, non-interference in each other's internal affairs, equality and mutual benefit, and peaceful coexistence.

Our Party's *Juche* idea and our Government's independent foreign policy enjoy the active support and sympathy of the world people. With each day, more and more people throughout the world are expressing sympathy with our Party's revolutionary *Juche* idea, and positively supporting the principle of independence maintained by the Government of the Republic.

Today progressive people in the world want to live in accordance with the *Juche* idea and many countries demand independence. No one wants to be subjugated by others. No nation will tolerate interference in its internal affairs and infringement upon its dignity; not only the socialist countries but also the newly independent countries oppose foreign interference and restrictions, and are taking the road to independence and self-reliance. Even capitalist countries do not want to blindly follow big powers any longer but are demanding the right of independent actions. The world's people are now demanding the *Juche* idea and many countries are on the road of independence. This is an irresistible trend of our time.

You wanted to hear our views on peace in Viet Nam and the Asian policy of U.S. imperialism in this context. I will now touch on this problem briefly.

Peace has not yet been achieved and the war is still going on in Viet Nam. This is very regrettable not only for you but also for the Asian people and the peace-loving people the world over. Particularly, the war in Viet Nam is causing great misfortunes and sufferings to its people.

It is entirely because of the crafty and vicious U.S. imperialist policy of aggression that peace has not been achieved in Viet Nam.

As you know, in recent years U.S. imperialism has repeatedly sustained great setbacks in the Viet Nam war and has undergone a serious political economic and military crisis at home and abroad. To find a way out of this dead end, U.S. imperialism produced the so-called "Nixon doctrine." This is a more crafty and insidious policy of aggression aimed at making Asians fight Asians in Asia and Africans fight Africans in Africa.

However, the "Nixon doctrine" is a stereotyped and wornout artifice which is quite infeasible. The reactionary ruling circles have long employed it to save themselves whenever they are driven into a predicament.

Above all, the "Nixon doctrine" is going bankrupt in the face of the Vietnamese people's heroic war of resistance. At present, the U.S. imperialists, while persistently furthering the plan to "Vietnamize" the war in south Viet Nam, are more viciously committing the criminal acts of blockading the coast of the Democratic Republic of Viet Nam and indiscriminately bombing its towns, villages and economic and cultural establishments. But they continue to suffer heavy military and political setbacks in the face of the heroic struggle of the Vietnamese people, who have risen as one in the battle for national salvation against U.S. aggression.

In order to ensure peace in Viet Nam, the U.S. imperialists must immediately stop their aggressive war, give up the policy of "Vietnamization" of the war and get out of south Viet Nam, taking with them their armed forces of aggression, troops of their satellites and puppets and lethal weapons. The Viet Nam question must be solved by the Vietnamese people themselves without any interference from outside forces.

The heroic Vietnamese people who are enjoying the powerful support and encouragement of the revolutionary peoples of Asia and the rest of the world will frustrate the U.S. imperialist policy of "Vietnamization" and surely win great victory in their struggle to liberate the south, defend the north and reunify the country.

Now, I would like to refer briefly to the Government of the Republic's position on the discussion of the Korean question at the UN General Assembly this year.

At present we take a fundamentally different position to that of our enemy on this matter.

As they did last year, the U.S. imperialists and south Korean rulers are employing the tactics of stalling the discussion of the Korean question at the UN General Assembly this year. They maintain that there is no need for the UN General Assembly to deal with the Korean question and its discussion must be postponed because talks have begun between the Red Cross organizations of north and south Korea and dialogues are going on between the north and south.

This assertion is quite contrary to the will of the Korean people; it is an exremely unjust assertion aimed at hampering the independent, peaceful reunification of Korea. Sinister designs are hidden in the scheme of the U.S. imperialists and south Korean rulers to put off the consideration of the Korean question at the UN General Assembly again this year, on the pretext of the partial contacts and dialogues now going on between the north and south. By putting off the discussion, the U.S. imperialists try to cover up their policy of aggression in Korea, and the south Korean rulers want to keep the U.S. imperialist aggressor troops stationed in south Korea. Therefore, the tactics of the U.S. imperialists and south Korean rulers in relation to the United Nations are totally aggressive and antipopular.

To counter these enemy tactics, the Government of the Republic has decided to insist on the discussion of the Korean question at this year's UN General Assembly session.

We consider the United Nations should help the Korean people's struggle for the independent, peaceful reunification of their country because dialogues are being held between the north and south, the talks are going on between the Red Cross organizations of north and south Korea, and the north and south made a joint statement which calls for the unity of the Korean nation to reunify the country peacefully free from foreign interference.

If the United Nations wants to help toward the independent, peaceful reunification of Korea, it should not postpone but conduct the discussion of the Korean question at this year's UN General Assembly session. It should take positive steps in order that the Korean people's struggle to reunify their country peacefully on the principle of national self-determination may succeed.

The United Natons must first dissolve the "UN Commission for the Unification and Rehabilitation of Korea," take the cap of "UN forces" off the U.S. imperialist aggressor army occupying south Korea under the UN signboard and force them to withdraw from south Korea. At the same time, it must revoke all the resolutions and actions against the Korean people's struggle for national reunification, and adopt a resolution for the independent, peaceful reunification of Korea. If the United Nations takes these measures, Korea's peaceful reunification will stand a better chance of coming about

Many countries are supporting our policy toward the United Nations today. More and more countries will give support to our just policy in the future.

We consider that with the active support of the world's progressive people, the United Nations will, sooner or later, take positive measures for the independent, peaceful reunification of Korea.

3. On the Question of the Peaceful Reunification of Korea

It is the invariable policy of our Party and the Government of the Republic to reunify the divided country independently and peacefully. From the first days of our country's division, we have made every sincere effort for its peaceful reunification.

However, our country still remains divided into the north and south; it has not been reunified though 27 years have passed since liberation. Our people who are suffering from territorial division and a nation split unanimously want the peaceful reunification of the country.

The aspiration for peaceful national reunification is rising rapidly, not only among the people in the northern half of the Republic, but among the south Korean people.

When the sentiments for peaceful reunification were rapidly mounting among the south Korean people, we declared in the August 6 speech last year that we were ready to come in contact, at any time, with all political parties including the Democratic Republican Party, social organizations and individual personages in south Korea.

After we made this new proposal expressing our readiness to get in contact even with the Democratic Republican Party of south Korea, the south Korean people increased their pressure and the world raised its voice for such a contact. This compelled the south Korean authorities to propose to hold north-south Red Cross talks and start a movement to search for families. Needless to say, we had proposed political negotiations with the south Korean side. But since we have consistently desired to have north-south contact ever since right after liberation, we valued their proposal despite its limitations and agreed to hold talks, though confined to a movement to search for families. As a result, the preliminary talks between the Red Cross organizations of the north and south opened on September 20 last year.

When the preliminary talks opened, the south Korean people, to say nothing of the people in the northern half of the Republic, deeply rejoiced over the materialization of north-south contacts and warmly hailed it with great excitement. Following the preliminary talks between the Red Cross organizations of the north and south, the sentiments for peaceful reunification mounted still higher among the south Korean people.

Scared by the south Korean people's fast-mounting sentiments for peaceful reunification, the south Korean authorities proclaimed a "state of emergency" under the fictitious pretext of "threat of southward aggression from the north" and launched the racket of suppressing the people. The declaration of the "state of emergency" by the south Korean rulers was merely a deceptive manoeuvre to dampen the sentiments for peaceful reunification and the democratic aspiration rapidly growing among the south Korean people.

Even after they declared the "state of emergency," we put forward different positive proposals for reunification, out of the desire to dispel the dark clouds of the national split and reunify the country in a peaceful way.

The pressure of the south Korean people, and the strong opinion of the people of the world, forced the south Korean authorities to propose secret north-south high-level talks separately from the preliminary talks between the Red Cross organizations of the north and south. Thus, as is known to the world, the north south high-level talks were held and the North-South Joint Statement was made public with our three principles of national reunification as its main content.

The high-level talks between the north and south and the North-South Joint Statement have opened up a bright prospect for our nation in its struggle to bring about the independent, peaceful reunification of the country. The spirit of the North-South Joint Statement on the peaceful reunification of the country by the efforts of the Koreans themselves, free from foreign interference, has evoked the sympathy of all the Korean people, and the world at large.

However, the announcement of the North-South Joint Statement does not mean that all problems of national reunification will be solved easily. In order to achieve the independent, peaceful reunification of the country, all the Korean people must carry on their consistent struggle with patience.

After the joint statement was made, the south Korean authorities turned their backs and are now employing a double dealing tactic; they are not honestly implementing the agreements stipulated in the joint statement. They say good words when they have face-to-face talks with us. But as soon as they turn on their heels, they slander us and become engrossed in statements and acts contrary to the fundamental spirit of the joint statement.

The first principle of national reunification made clear in the North-South Joint Statement is to reunify the country independently on the principle of national self-determination, without relying on outside forces or their interference. Frankly speaking, reunifying the country independently means forcing U.S. imperialism out of south Korea and preventing other foreign forces from interfering in the reunification of our country.

We are in alliance with the Soviet Union and China, but they do not meddle in the internal affairs of our country. There are neither Soviet troops nor Chinese People's Volunteers in our country. The outside forces now encroaching upon our sovereignty and standing in the way of our national reunification are none other than U.S. imperialism and some Japanese reactionaries. In order to reunify the country independently, therefore, we must oppose U.S. imperialism and Japanese militarism, which are interfering in the internal affairs of our country.

Nevertheless, the south Korean authorities, even after they agreed to the principle of independent national reunification, are still making absurd allegations that the United Nations is not an outside force, that U.S. troops should remain in south Korea for a long time or that Korea should be reunified through UN-supervised elections.

The North-South Joint Statement also affirms the principle that national reunification should be attained by peaceful means, without recourse to force of arms against each other. If this principle is to be observed, both sides must refrain from words and deeds that would aggravate the situation.

We have clearly stated more than once that we have no intention to "invade the south." But the south Korean rulers say that they cannot trust our statements, and they are clamoring that they must "build up strength" for north-south confrontation by reinforcing military installations both at the front and in the rear and speeding up modernization of armaments. They are also staging military exercises more frequently. This is a grave act that will aggravate tension between the north and south.

The south Korean rulers' preposterous vilifications and provocations against us are evoking resentment among our people and People's Army and creating a tension within the dialogue after all. This act will only help produce an atmosphere of war rather than an atmosphere of reunification.

Another major principle of national reunification clarified in the North-South Joint Statement is that of promoting the great unity of the nation transcending the differences in ideology, ideal and social system.

If we do not force the socialist system of the northern half upon south Korea and the south Korean authorities do not force us to restore the capitalist system, why should we, one and the same nation, fight against each other? We are not forcing socialism upon south Korea. What society south Korea will be in the future, will be decided by the south Korean people according to their own will. The south Korean rulers are now clamoring that a "wind of freedom" should be sent into the north. This arrogant attitude is aimed at obstructing peaceful reunification.

The principle of achieving the great national unity transcending the differences in ideology, ideal and social system demands the democratization of society and the freedom of political activities for all parties, all groupings and personages of all strata. Only when society is democratized, can all the forces desirous of the independent, peaceful reunification of the country be united in one, irrespective of the differences in ideas, political views, religious beliefs and political groupings.

Even after the announcement of the North-South Joint Statement, however, the south Korean authorities have been suppressing democratic freedom as ever and intensifying their fascist repression of the people, claiming that there is no reason to revise the "Anti-Communist Law" and the "National Security Law." They are even restricting the activities of the opposition, and are preventing the opposition party members from making contact with us. They are arresting and imprisoning many people who advocated contact and interchange between the north and south and national reunification on charges of violating the "Anti-Communist Law." Some time ago the south Korean authorities went so far as to execute the patriots who had striven for democracy and peaceful reunification in south Korea. This is a naked provocation to us.

Though they solemnly pledged the nation to conscientiously carry out the agreements in the joint statement, the south Korean rulers are thus violating them without hesitation. They do not think of the consequences of their treachery to the nation.

These provocative acts of the south Korean authorities are

infuriating the entire Korean people, and the world's people as well. For the sake of national reunification we are restraining our indignation and showing patience to the arrogant gangsterism on the part of the south Korean rulers. Their acts will, in the long run, evoke greater wrath among all the Korean people.

If the south Korean authorities desist from such acts, observe the provisions of the North-South Joint Statement, the main content of which is the three principles of national reunification, make efforts to remove distrust and achieve mutual understanding, and make sincere efforts for the solution of the reunification question, we will continue to work patiently for the independent, peaceful reunification of the country.

First of all, we will exert every effort to bring about the earliest possible success of the talks between the Red Cross organizations of the north and south now going on amid the expectations of the whole nation. In this way we intend to alleviate the misfortunes and hardships of the families and relatives separated in the north and south by the artificial division of the country, and provide favorable conditions for the independent, peaceful reunification of the country.

Along with this, we will form and operate the North-South Co-ordination Commission as soon as possible, in order to implement the provisions of the North-South Joint Statement and so solve various problems to expedite the country's reunification.

However, the question of the country's reunification cannot be fully solved merely through contacts and negotiations in such a limited scope as the north-south Red Cross talks and the North-South Co-ordination Commission. The reunification of the country involves many problems which cannot be solved within the functions of the north-south Red Cross talks or the North-South Co-ordination Commission. To settle fundamental problems for the country's reunification, it is necessary to have contacts and negotiations on a wider scale, and in many more fields, to discuss a number of specific measures for removing the long-accumulated misunderstanding and mistrust between the north and south, promoting understanding and attaining independent, peaceful reunification. That is why we insist on immediately holding political negotiations, such as a joint conference of political parties and social organizations in north and south Korea, or a conference of the north and south Korean authorities, or a joint conference of our Supreme People's Assembly deputies and the south Korean "national assemblymen."

In order to attain the peaceful reunification of the country as early as possible we deem it necessary to institute a north-south Confederation for the present.

The north-south Confederation we propose, involves the formation of a supreme national council with representatives of the Government of the Democratic People's Republic of Korea and the "Government of the Republic of Korea" to solve political, economic, military and cultural problems arising between the north and south and thereby attain national unity, while maintaining the present political systems of the north and south as they are. There is the difference in system between them. But if both the north and south abide by the principle of not forcing their social systems on each other, there will be no reasons why they should not institute a north-south Confederation.

Once the Confederation is established, there will be more contacts and visits and economic and cultural intercourses will also be effected more smoothly between the north and south. If the north and south economically work together and conduct interchange it will be possible to rapidly improve the economic situation of south Korea by utilizing the developed heavy industry and rich underground resources in the northern half of the Republic and it will greatly benefit the people in both parts of Korea. Sportsmen and artists may visit the north and south having sports games and giving art performances, and form single north-south teams and single art troupes to participate in international sports competitions and international art festivals. Journalists may also freely travel for news coverage; and it will be possible to set up press centers of newspaper bureaus in Pyongyang and Seoul and exchange newspapers and journals between the north and south.

If a north-south Confederation is instituted and broad intercourses and visits are effected in economic, cultural and all other domains, mistrust and cold feeling between the north and south will be removed and a climate of mutual understanding and trust be created, and national unity can be easily attained. If an atmosphere of trust is created and national unity achieved between the north and south, the independent, peaceful reunification of the country will be actualized by way of establishing an all-Korea unified government through north-south general elections on a democratic basis, without any interference of outside forces.

4. On the Relations Between Korea and Japan

As you know, in those days of the Sato Cabinet, the Japanese government pursued an extremely hostile policy toward our country. But there is an indication that the present Tanaka Cabinet is pursuing a little less hostile policy than the Sato Cabinet. Sato obdurately opposed the travels of Korean citizens in Japan to and from the homeland and their trips abroad. Korean citizens in Japan are now allowed to make trips abroad to some extent and they are permitted to visit their homeland, though partially. I think this is a good thing.

However, we cannot say that everything has been settled in the relations between Korea and Japan. Many problems have yet to be solved in order to normalize relations between the two countries.

To form a friendly relationship and establish normal diplomatic relations between Korea and Japan, the Japanese government must first change its attitude toward our country. It is entirely because of the hostile policy of the Japanese government that friendly relations have not been formed till today between Korea and Japan. If the Japanese government stops meddling in the internal affairs of the Korean peninsula and takes a friendly attitude toward our country, everything will be settled smoothly between Korea and Japan.

Our position on the question of Korea-Japan relations is consistent. From the first days, the Democratic People's Republic of Korea has hoped to have good-neighbor relations with Japan even though its social system differs from ours. Even now, we want to put an end to the abnormal situation between the two countries as early as practicable and establish normal relations.

If the Japanese government is desirous of establishing good-neighbor relations with our country, it should renounce the one-sided policy and adopt an unbiased policy devoid of aggressive aim to both the north and south of the Korean peninsula; and by doing so, it should help toward accelerating Korean reunification.

Pursuing the one-sided policy, the Japanese government is trying to sow the seed of discord in the Korean peninsula by egging on one side to oppose the other. This is most undesirable. The Japanese government should hope that the Korean peninsula, its neighbor, will become stable, and north and south Korea will be reunified and live in peace and happiness. If people in the next-door house were in turmoil and fighting each other, it would not benefit Japan either, would it? We consider that for its own benefit, too, the Japanese government should pursue a friendly policy toward our country, its neighbor.

It is true that there is a difference in the systems of our country and Japan. But we think that it would be quite correct for the Japanese government to treat our country on an equal footing and establish diplomatic relations with us on the five principles of peaceful coexistence, since it has established diplomatic relations with other countries with different social systems.

Even before the establishment of diplomatic relations with Japan, we are ready to effect frequent visits of journalists, technicians and other sectors of people and conduct broad economic and cultural interchange. This sort of intercourse must not be one-sided; it must be conducted on the principles of equality and mutual benefit.

As you know, Korea and Japan are conducting some interchange at present. However, it cannot but assume a one-sided character because of the unfriendly attitude of the Japanese government. Take the exchange of journalists for example. You Japanese journalists can visit our country but our journalists cannot visit Japan. As long as this one-sided intercourse is conducted, friendly relations will never develop between the two countries.

In our opinion, whether good-neighbor relations will be established between Korea and Japan or not depends entirely on the Japanese government's attitude, aside from specific procedures.

In the establishment of friendly relations between Korea and Japan it is very important that the Japanese government guarantees the Korean citizens in Japan their national rights.

Foreigners should be guaranteed their national rights. This is the requirement of international law. But the Korean citizens in Japan are not given a treatment due to foreigners today although they have the nationality of the Democratic People's Republic of Korea. This is another expression of the Japanese government's unfriendly attitude toward our country.

We demand that, first of all, the Korean citizens in Japan be guaranteed the full right to national education, as well as the right to repatriation, and the freedom of travel to and from the homeland.

You said that Japan has incurred widespread criticism internationally by its rapid economic development in recent years and asked for our views of Japan's present situation and foreign policy. Let me make a brief remark on this point.

We do not think ill of Japan's economic development. Why should we think ill of our neighbor's economic development? If the development of Japan's economy is not used for the revival of militarism and aggression on other countries and contributes to enhancing the material and cultural living standards of the Japanese people and promoting its friendly relations with other countries, it will indeed be a good thing.

In the past, however, the reactionary Japanese ruling circles craftily schemed to speed up the militarization of the country and invade other countries on the basis of revival of Japan's monopoly capital and the establishment of its ruling system. The Japanese reactionaries have not yet dispatched troops abroad, but are laying a stepping stone for their future military aggression in other countries. This shows the danger of the revival of Japanese militarism.

At present, the Japanese reactionaries, actively speeding up the militarization of the country, have made no scruple of embarking on the road of aggression against other countries, under the guise of being their "helper." Taking advantage of the economic difficulties of some countries in Southeast Asia, they try to seize the key branches of their economy by increasing the export of capital to these countries under various names such as "government loan," "direct investment" and "joint enterprise." They attach big political strings to their "economic aid" in an attempt to sway some new independent countries to the Right and deflect them from the anti-imperialist front.

Japan's reactionary ruling circles started their full scale economic infiltration into south Korea after manufacturing the criminal "ROK-Japan treaty." They are frantically working to reduce south Korea again into Japan's exclusive colony, stepping up political and military infiltration along with the economic infiltration.

It was reported that some time ago the Japanese authorities went to Seoul and held the "ROK-Japan ministerial conference" with the south Korean rulers, at which they agreed to conclude an "agreement on industrial ownership" with the south Korean reactionaries as a price of the so-called "aid." This is also an open act of aggression designed to subordinate south Korea to Japan economically. The conclusion of the "agreement on industrial ownership" between Japan and south Korea will enable the Japanese monopolies to have privileges in their business activities in south Korea, and will shackle the south Korean economy more tightly to the rapacious Japanese monopoly capital. This will create the danger of another Japanese invasion of south Korea, just as the Japanese imperialists invaded our country in 1894 under the pretext of protecting the Japanese property and the Japanese residents. As you see, Japanese monopoly capital is paving the way for overseas aggression of Japanese militarism.

This is why our people are becoming more vigilant against the fattening Japanese monopoly capital and resolutely fighting against the militarization of Japan's economy, and its overseas aggression.

The Japanese reactionaries must not forget the lesson of history and must stop the militarization of Japan's economy and manoeuvres for overseas aggression. If the Japanese reactionaries continue to take the road of overseas aggression, oblivious of the lesson of history, they will sustain another shameful defeat in face of the struggle of our people and the world's progressive people.

The Korean people express solidarity with the Japanese people in their righteous struggle against the revival of Japanese militarism and the Japanese reactionaries' aggressive manoeuvres.

I take this opportunity to send my greetings to the Japanese people and progressive men of the Japanese press who are helping the Korean citizens in Japan in their struggle to defend their democratic, national rights and actively surpporting our people's struggle for the independent, peaceful reunification of the country.

Let Us Prevent A National Split and Reunify the Country (*Excerpt*)

Speech at the Pyongyang Mass Rally to Welcome the
Party and Government Delegation of the Czechoslovak
Socialist Republic, June 23, 1973

Comrades and friends, today the international situation is developing in favor of socialism and the revolutionary forces and to the disadvantage of imperialism and the reactionary forces.

In the face of the growing forces of socialism and the national-liberation, working-class and democratic movements, imperialism is on the decline and is finding itself in a more difficult situation with each passing day. In an attempt to find a way out, the imperialists are resorting to craftier double-dealing tactics.

The United States is carrying on aggressive and interventionist activities in many parts of the world under the signboard of "peace," and trying to maintain its colonial domination by suppressing small nations by force while improving its relations with big ones.

This is fully proved by the U.S. manoeuvrings of aggression and intervention against Korea, Cambodia, Viet Nam, Laos, a number of Arab countries, Cuba and many other nations of the world.

The United States wants to take hold of south Korea forever, as a major stronghold to save its colonial ruling system which is going into total bankruptcy in Asia.

Adopting the double-faced tactics under the "Nixon doctrine," the United States is not willing to desist from its manoeuvrings to instigate south Korea's bellicose elements to make Koreans fight Koreans, perpetuate the division of Korea and create two Koreas, even after the North-South Joint Statement was made public and the dialogue started between the two parts of Korea.

In step with these U.S. machinations, the south Korean authorities are also employing double-dealing tactics. They are scheming to perpetuate the division of the nation and exerting all efforts to reinforce their military strength, putting up the signboard of "peaceful reunification" on the one hand and, on the other, openly clamoring for "confrontation with dialogue," "competition with dialogue" and "coexistence with dialogue."

Because of all this the dialogue between the north and south of Korea is not making progress the way it should and a big stumbling block still lies in the way to reunification, despite the consistent, sincere efforts of our Party and the Government of our Republic for the country's independent, peaceful reunification. Consequently the bright prospect for national reunification which was opened before our nation when the historic North-South Joint Statement was published a year ago is being blighted.

Out of our earnest desire to get over the difficult situation created today and materialize the people's long-cherished aspiration for peaceful national reunification as soon as possible, we hereby reaffirm before the world the policy of our Party and the Government of our Republic for independent, peaceful reunification:

1. To improve the present relations between the north and south of Korea and accelerate the peaceful reunification of the country, it is

*necessary, first of all, to eliminate military confrontation and ease ten-
sion between north and south.*

To remove military confrontation and alleviate tension between the north and south is a matter of pressing urgency and
vital importance at present in dispelling the misunderstanding
and mistrust, and deepening mutual understanding and trust
between the north and south, creating the atmosphere for a
great national unity, ameliorating the relations between the
north and south, and bringing about the peaceful reunification
of the country.

The military confrontation between the north and south with
huge armed forces itself constitutes not only a major factor that
menaces peace in our country but also a source of misunderstanding and mistrust.

Only when this fundamental question is solved can tension
and mistrust between the north and south be removed, the
climate of trust be created, and all problems be settled successfully on the basis of mutual trust. It is unnatural to advocate the
peaceful reunification and hold a dialogue, with a dagger in
one's bosom. Unless the dagger is taken out and laid down, it is
impossible to create an atmosphere of mutual trust or find satis-
factory solutions to any problems, big and small, related to the
country's reunfication, including that of achieving the collaboration and interchange between the north and south .

Therefore, as the first step for the peaceful reunification of the
country, we have more than once advanced to the south Korean
authorities the five-point proposal: To cease the reinforcement
of armies and arms race, make all foreign troops withdraw,
reduce armed forces and armaments, stop the introduction of
weapons from abroad and to conclude a peace agreement.

Nevertheless, the south Korean authorities want to put off the
solution of this urgent problem and gradually solve matters of
secondary importance through different stages. Actually this is
intended not to increase mutual trust and promote great national unity, but to maintain and freeze the territorial division,
keeping the painful wound of national partition unhealed.

If they truly desire the peaceful reunification and seek the practical solution of the reunification question, the south Korean authorities must renounce this position and take the course of removing military confrontation.

2. To improve the north-south relations and expedite the country's reunification, it is necessary to materialize many-sided collaboration and interchange between the north and the south in the political, military, diplomatic, economic and cultural fields.

The many-sided collaboration and interchange between the north and south are of tremendous importance in rejoining the severed ties of the nation and providing preconditions for reunification. Only when such collaboration and interchange are actualized, will it be possible to consolidate the peace agreement to be concluded between the north and south.

The south Korean authorities propose in words that both sides "completely open" their societies to each other, but in actual fact they are afraid of tearing down any of the barriers between the north and south and dead set against the interchange and collaboration between the two parts of the country.

The south Korean authorities are not collaborating with fellow countrymen now. In collusion with outside forces, they are bringing in foreign monopoly capital without limit to reduce the south Korean economy completely to a dependent economy. They are even spoiling our beautiful land by introducing the pollutional industries which are rejected as "rubbish" in foreign countries.

We again emphasize that if the south Korean authorities have a spark of national conscience, they should strive to develop the economy in the interests of our nation through the joint exploitation of our country's natural resources, and bring about national collaboration in all spheres.

3. In order to settle the question of the country's reunification in conformity with the will and demand of our people, it is necessary to enable the masses of people of all strata in the north and south to participate in the nationwide patriotic work for national reunification.

We consider that the dialogue between the north and south for national reunification should not be confined to the authorities of the north and south, but be held on a nationwide scale.

To this end, we propose to convene a Great National Congress composed of representatives of people of all walks of life—the workers, working peasants, working intellectuals, student youths and soldiers in the north, and the workers, peasants, student youths, intellectuals, military personnel, national capitalists and petty bouregeoisie in south Korea—and the representatives of political parties and social organizations in the north and south, and comprehensively discuss and solve the question of the country's reunification at this Congress.

4. What is of great significance today in speeding up the country's reunification is to institute a north-south Confederation under the name of a single country.

It goes without saying that there may be various ways to materialize the complete reunification of the country.

Under the prevailing conditions we think that the most reasonable way for the reunification is to convene the Great National Congress and achieve national unity, and on this basis, institute the north-south Confederation, leaving the two existing social systems in the north and south as they are for the time being.

In case the north-south Confederation is instituted, it will be good to name this confederal state Confederal Republic of Koryo, after Koryo, a unitary state which once existed on our territory and was widely known to the world. This will be a good name for the state acceptable both to the north and south.

The founding of the Confederal Republic of Koryo will open up a decisive phase in preventing a national split, bringing about all-round contact and collaboration between the north and south, and in hastening the complete reunification.

5. *We consider that our country should be prevented from being split into two Koreas permanently as a result of the freezing of national division and that the north and south should also work together in the field of external activity.*

Of course we are developing state relations with all countries friendly to our Republic on the principle of equality and mutual benefit; but we resolutely oppose all machinations designed to make use of this to manufacture two Koreas.

We hold that the north and south should not enter the UN separately, and consider that if they want to enter the UN before the reunification of the country, they should enter it as a single state under the name of the Confederal Republic of Koryo, at least after the Confederation is set up.

But apart from the question of admission to the UN, if the Korean question is placed on its agenda for discussion, the representative of our Republic should be entitled to take part in it and speak as the party concerned.

Our people are a single people who have lived with the same culture and the same language through many centuries, and they can never live separated in two parts.

Our proposal is to remove military confrontation and ease tension between the north and south, materialize many-sided collaboration and interchange between the two parts, convene the Great National Congress composed of representatives of people of all strata and political parties and social organizations in the north and south, institute the north-south Confederation under the single name of the Confederal Republic of Koryo and enter the UN under the single name of the Confederal Republic of Koryo. When this proposal for the country's reunification is put into effect, there will be a great turning point in accomplishing the historic cause of peaceful national reunification on the principle of the North-South Joint Statement, as commonly desired by our people and the world's people.

We expect the south Korean authorities to approach this new fair proposal of ours for reunification with sincerity.

At the same time we strongly demand that the United States must look straight at the fast changing situation of today, withdraw its troops from south Korea as soon as practicable and discontinue its aggressions and interventions against our country.

If the United States thinks that it can swallow up small nations one by one, while improving its relations only with big powers, or maintain its colonial domination by propping up its minions forsaken by the people under the signboard of "anti-communism," it is gravely mistaken. Such policies of the United States will rather arouse the resistance and hatred of the majority of the world's people and hasten its ruin.

We think that now the UN should deal a blow to the United States' manoeuvre to justify the occupation of south Korea by its troops under the pretext of the UN "resolution."

The UN must take the "UN forces" helmets off the U.S. troops in south Korea, make them withdraw, and dissolve the "United Nations Commission for the Unification and Rehabilitation of Korea," and thus remove all obstacles it has laid to hamper the independent, peaceful reunification of Korea. This is in keeping with the trend of the present times toward independence and peace. This is demanded by the general situation of the world.

It is none other than the Japanese militarists, who are still working desperately in the international arena as the most active followers of the U.S. imperialists in their bankrupt machination to meddle in our internal affairs. We again warn the Japanese militarists that they must also look squarely at reality, give up their hostile policy against the Democratic People's Republic of Korea and desist from their crafty manoeuvres to seize an opportunity to actualize their wild desire for invading south Korea again.

Answers To The Questions Raised By L'Unita, Organ Of The Italian Communist Party *(Excerpt)*

January 29, 1974

Question: One year ago we heard with a great hope that an agreement was reached between the two parts of Korea on peacefully reunifying the country, free from interference of outside forces. But, later we learned that new difficulties cropped up in its way.

Will you please tell us what these difficulties are and how they can be overcome?

Answer: In 1972 a North-South Joint Statement whose keynote is the three principles of independence, peaceful reunification and great national unity put forward by our Party, was made public in our country as a result of the dialogue held between the north and the south. This was a big advance in the struggle of our people for the independent, peaceful reunification of their fatherland. The people throughout the world, to say nothing of the entire Korean people in the north and the south, rejoiced and warmly hailed it.

After the announcement of the North-South Joint Statement we made every possible effort to put it into practice and achieve national reunification as early as possible. But in this effort we ran up against a big obstacle owing to the manoeuvres of the domestic and foreign splitters to perpetuate national division.

The south Korean authorities, manipulated by US imperialism, scrapped the North-South Joint Statement on the day following its signature, saying that it was no more than an untrustworthy piece of paper. After that, they kept perpetrating acts totally contravening the principles of the North-South Joint Statement and turned down all the reasonable proposals we put forward to accelerate national reunification. Then, last June, they openly announced to the world a "policy" of fixing and perpetuating the national division. The south Korean authorities asserted that north and south Korea should enter the United Nations separately. This was designed, in the last analysis, to freeze the division of the nation and keep our country divided into two parts forever.

The nation-splitting manoeuvres of the south Korean authorities are a product of the "two Koreas" policy of US imperialism. Seeing that it was impossible to materialize their wild design to invade the northern half of the Republic and turn the whole of Korea into their colony, the US imperialists brought forward the "two Koreas" policy with the sinister aim of keeping at least south Korea in their grip. At the United Nations General Assembly session last year the US imperialists, together with their followers, resorted to all sorts of tricks to pass a "resolution" on "two Koreas".

The Japanese militarists most zealously follow the US imperialists in their "two Koreas" plot. While stepping up their renewed invasion of south Korea, the Japanese militarists, hand and glove with the US imperialists, are actively pushing ahead with the plot to create "two Koreas". It is not for nothing that some time ago a Japanese journal wrote that "the 'two Koreas' policy is a drama acted by the Pak Jung Hi regime of a US script, under US direction and Japanese stage management".

We consider that the road to the solution of our country's reunification question can be cleared only by smashing the "two Koreas" plot of the US imperialists, the Japanese militarists and the south Korean authorities and by putting an end to foreign interference in the Korean question.

The Workers' Party of Korea and the Government of the Republic resolutely oppose any attempt to fix and perpetuate the division of our country and thoroughly reject any outside interference in the domestic affairs of our country.

Last year's session of the United Nations General Assembly, the historically first to be held with the attendance of the representative of the Democratic People's Republic of Korea, checked the "two Koreas" plot of US imperialism and its lackeys, expressed support to the three principles of national reunification laid down in the North-South Joint Statement and adopted a decision on the immediate dissolution of the "United Nations Commission for the Unification and Rehabilitation of Korea", a tool of US imperialism for its interference in our internal affairs. This was a welcome step which created a favorable situation for the solution of our country's reunification question and a great victory of our Party's policy of independent, peaceful reunification.

The Workers' Party of Korea and the Government of the Republic will make every possible effort as ever for smashing all attempts to perpetuate the division of our nation and hastening the independent, peaceful reunification of the fatherland.

First of all, we will actively struggle to strip the "UN forces" cap off the US imperialist aggression force in south Korea, the main obstacle to the solution of Korea's reunification question, and to force it to withdraw. At the same time, we will strive to continue the dialogue between the north and the south and to realize a many-sided collaboration and interchange between them in accordance with the principles clarified in the North-South Joint Statement.

In order to continue and develop the dialogue between the north and the south, the south Korean authorities must refrain from any acts contravening the principles of the North-South Joint Statement. They are still now persisting in the manoeuvres to perpetuate the national division and the policy of dependence upon outside forces. They are harshly repressing the democratic personalities and patriotic youth and students of south Korea who call for national reunification and democracy. Today such acts of the south Korean authorities constitute the chief obstacle to the dialogue between the north and the south.

If the south Korean authorities renounce their splitting stand, respect the North-South Joint Statement and make sincere efforts for its implementation, the north-south dialogue will make a successful progress.

If the south Korean authorities continue to ignore the North-South Joint Statement and follow the road which runs counter to it, the people will not pardon them. The south Korean youth, students and people, indignant at the south Korean authorities' ever more undisguised policy of fascist repression and manoeuvres to perpetuate the national split and their policy of dependence upon Japan, have risen in the anti-"government" and anti-fascist struggle for democracy. For months now they have been valiantly fighting under the slogans: "Down with the Pak regime!" "Establish democracy!" and "An immediate end to dependence on Japan!" It is natural that the south Korean youth, students and people should struggle against those who, clinging to the sleeves of outside forces, betray the nation and repress the people by force.

The just, patriotic struggle of the south Korean youth, students and people will certainly be crowned with victory, and the cause of national reunification will surely be realized through the united strength of the entire Korean people.

Answers To Questions Put By The Chief Editor Of The Yugoslav Newspaper Vecernje Novosti

February 22, 1974

Question: Yugoslavia knows well and supports the consistent efforts of the Government of the Democratic People's Republic of Korea for the country's independent and peaceful reunification.

Would you please tell me of the present political situation in the context of the dialogue between the north and the south and of the prospect of Korean reunification?

Answer: As you know, as a result of the persevering efforts of our Party and the Government of the Republic for the country's independent and peaceful reunification, the dialogue started between the north and the south of Korea and in July 1972 the North-South Joint Statement was made public with the three principles of independence, peaceful reunification and great national unity as its keynote.

After the announcement of the North-South Joint Statement the Government of our Republic put forward a number of specific and reasonable proposals to translate it into practice and made all sincere efforts for the successful progress of the

213

dialogue. However, owing to the manoeuvres of the splitters within and without, the north-south dialogue has been dead-locked and great difficulties and obstacles have been laid in the way of the reunification of the fatherland.

Even after the announcement of the North-South Joint State-ment the south Korean authorities, instigated by the United States, intensified war preparations and fascist repression, more stubbornly sticking to the policy of dependence on outside forces in total contravention of the principles clarified in the statement. Then, in June last year, they made public the so-called "special statement", declaring to the world a "policy" to perpetuate the division of the nation.

At the UN General Assembly last year the US and Japanese reactionaries and the south Korean authorities put forward a proposal for simultaneous UN membership for "two Koreas" and employed every conceivable trick to force it through. But this scheme was completely frustrated by the just struggle of the socialist countries, non-aligned states and many other countries of the world which support our Party's policy of independent and peaceful reunification. The UN General Assembly expres-sed full support to the three principles of national reunification laid down in the North-South Joint Statement and adopted a resolution on the dissolution of the "United Nations Commis-sion for the Unification and Rehabilitation of Korea," a US in-strument for aggression and interference in another's internal affairs. This is a great victory for the policy of our Party and the Government of the Republic for independent and peaceful reunification and a staggering defeat for those who seek the permanent division of Korea.

The south Korean authorities' manoeuvres to perpetuate the division of the nation at the instigation of the imperialist forces have caused national indignation of the entire Korean people who aspire for the reunification of the fatherland and have in-evitably roused them to the struggle against the splitters within and without.

Harsh as fascist repression is today, the south Korean student youth and personages of all strata are valiantly fighting to bring about the democratization of south Korean society, save the country and the people and reunify the fatherland.

We put forward the five-point proposition: to remove the military confrontation and ease the tension between the north and the south, to materialize many-sided collaboration and exchange between the north and the south, to convoke a Great National Congress comprising representatives of people of all strata, political parties and social organizations in the north and the south, to institute a north-south Confederation under the single name of the Confederal Republic of Koryo and to enter the UN under the single name—the Confederal Republic of Koryo. This is an epochal save-the-nation plan aimed at preventing the division of the nation and reunifying the fatherland.

The only obstacle to the solution of the question of our country's reunification today is the manoeuvres of the splitters, within and without, to keep our nation indefinitely divided. If the question of our country's reunification is to be solved smoothly, an end must be put first to the "two Koreas" plot of the US and Japanese reactionaries and their interference in Korea's domestic affairs and the south Korean authorities must renounce the policy of dependence on outside forces and honestly observe the principles of the North-South Joint Statement. The south Korean authorities must discontinue their fascist repression of the south Korean people who demand democracy and the country's independent and peaceful reunification and open the way for representatives of all parties, groupings and people of all strata in south Korea to participate directly in the solution of the question of reunification. Only then will the dialogue between the north and the south make smooth progress and the solution of the question of the country's reunification be quickly facilitated.

Because of foreign interference we are now going through turns and twists in the solution of the question of the country's reunification. However, we will definitively win the cause of national reunification through an indefatigable united struggle of all the north and south Korean people with the active support and encouragement of the progressive people the world over.

Availing myself of this opportunity, I would like to express my deep thanks to the Government of the Socialist Federal Republic of Yugoslavia and the Yugoslav people for their active support to the DPRK Government's policy for independent and peaceful reunification and to the Korean people's struggle to put it into effect.

The Peoples of the Third World Who Advance Under the Uplifted Banner of Independence Will Certainly Win Their Revolutionary Cause *(Excerpt)*

Speech at Pyongyang Mass Rally in Welcome of Algerian President Houari Boumedienne, March 4, 1974

In the struggle for the achievement of the country's reunification, the long-cherished desire of our nation, we have maintained all along an independent stand for solving our national problem by ourselves, decisively rejecting the attempts to rely on outside forces.

Today the Korean question, after all, boils down to the question of whether reunification or division; whether one Korea or two Koreas.

The entire Korean people are unanimous in desiring the reunification of their country.

But the great powers want the division of our country. To divide and rule is an old method of imperialism.

The U.S. imperialists and the Japanese militarists seek the

217

permanent division of Korea, the former to reduce south Korea to their permanent colony and military base, and the latter to take hold of south Korea as their permanent commodity market.

Huge obstacles are still lying in the way of the reunification of our country even after the publication of the July 4 North-South Joint Statement, owing to the U.S. and Japanese reactionaries' manoeuvres of intervention and their stooges' treacheries to the country and nation.

In these days the nation-splitting machinations of the south Korean rulers and their provocations against the northern half of the Republic have reached a most intolerable level.

The south Korean rulers are intensifying their fascist suppression of the south Korean people as never before, arresting and imprisoning at random south Korean youths and students, conscientious intellectuals, and even religious figures on charges of demanding peaceful reunification. They are turning the whole of south Korea into a horrible prison.

In an effort to cover up their criminal acts and divert the attention of the people elsewhere, the south Korean rulers have committed such premeditated military provocations as the spy ship infiltration in the West Sea. Trying to capitalize on it, they are raising a wholesale clamor about the "threat of southward aggression" and deliberately increasing tensions between the north and the south.

It must not be overlooked that the U.S. imperialists, in step with the provocations of south Korean bellicose elements, send one high-speed, high-altitude reconnaissance plane after another into the air above the northern half of the Republic to commit espionage acts; and openly declare that they will further increase military aid to south Korea.

This ill-omened state of things in our country suggests that the splitters within and without are, in fact, leading the north-south relations back to the state before the announcement of the North-South Joint Statement and driving the situation to the brink of war.

It has become all the clearer now who in Korea is whetting the sword of aggression under the cloak of "peace" and who is seeking the perpetuation of split under the cloak of "unification."

Those who love the country and the nation should not tolerate the machinations of the U.S. and Japanese reactionaries to convert south Korea into a permanent colony, but compel the U.S. troops to get out of south Korea, thwart the Japanese militarists' invasion, and actively turn out to build a sovereign, reunified and independent Korea.

What is the use of holding the north-south dialogue, if our nation is to live divided? The north-south dialogue must be conducted, under any circumstances, for the purpose of achieving the reunification.

If the south Korean authorities really want the reunification, they should retract the "special statement" of June, 1973 advocating the membership of two Koreas for the United Nations and approach the talks for reunification in conformity with the interests of the whole nation.

They should not bring forward such a thing as a "non-aggression pact" devoid of any guarantee for peace, but accept our proposal for concluding a peace agreement.

The so-called "non-aggression pact" brought forward by the south Korean authorities some time ago is nothing but one designed to flout the nation's will on the question of reunification.

As the whole world knows, it is not the south Korean authorities but the U.S. army commander, under the mantle of the "United Nations commander," who holds the prerogative of the supreme command of the army in south Korea. It is also the U.S. imperialists who have control over the guns, rifles and all other means of war.

Under these conditions it is utterly ridiculous for the empty-handed south Korean rulers to propose us to conclude a "non-aggression pact," leaving the U.S. imperialist aggressor forces to stay in south Korea. Their proposal is not worth discussing at all.

The continued machinations of the south Korean authorities to maintain division lead us to disbelieve that they came to the dialogue for the purpose of reunification.

That is why we think that for its peaceful solution the question of reunification of the country should not be discussed only between the authorities of the north and south, but be referred to the entire nation for discussion.

In this connection, we propose, once again, to convene a great national congress or a north-south political consultative conference participated in by the representatives of all political parties and public organizations and personages of all strata in the north and south, apart from the existing North-South Coordination Commission. This is the only way for realizing the reunification of Korea.

The question of Korea's reunification should be settled by the Koreans themselves; it cannot be solved for us by any big powers or any other countries.

The present situation urgently demands of us to further intensify the struggle against the splitters in order to prevent the division of the country and realize the peaceful reunification of the country.

This is a struggle to decide whether we save the country or betray it.

If the south Korean authorities reject the independent and peaceful reunification of the country and attempt to fabricate two Koreas, persistently clinging to the policy of dependence upon outside forces, they will meet their destruction, with the disgrace of traitors never to be washed off from their names.

The south Korean people are now fighting courageously for freedom and democratic rights and the independent and peaceful reunification of the country. They are not yielding to the harsh fascist suppression by the south Korean rulers.

The struggle of the south Korean people is a patriotic struggle for saving the country and the nation and reunifying the fatherland. It is a just struggle directly related to the vital interests of the nation.

That is why our Party and the Government of our Republic will always actively support the revolutionary struggle of the south Korean people with might and main.

Our support to the revolutionary struggle of the south Korean people is by no means an "interference in other's internal affairs," rather it is for solving, by ourselves, the internal affairs of our nation.

As one and the same nation, we regard it as our natural duty to support the revolutionary struggle of the south Korean people.

In order to remove the tensions and prevent war in Korea, the U.S. imperialists and the Japanese militarists should not defend the present south Korean authorities who are indulging in fascist repression and war provocation manoeuvres but desist from their interference in the internal affairs of our country.

Our people's struggle for national reunification enjoys ever greater support and sympathy in the international arena, being an important link in the world-wide anti-imperialist national liberation struggle.

A resolution fully conforming to our five-point program of national reunification was unanimously adopted at the Fourth Summit Conference of Non-Aligned States in Algeria last year. This was convincing proof that our people's struggle for national reunification enjoyed the full support of the world progressive people.

Under this world trend the United Nations General Assembly last year rejected the moves of the United States and the south Korean authorities for the admission of "two Koreas" to the United Nations, designed for perpetuation of the division of Korea and adopted a decision on dissolving the "United Nations Commission for the Unification and Rehabilitation of Korea," the U.S. imperialists' tool of aggression.

This is a great victory for our people and a common victory for peace-loving people of the world.

We express the conviction that in the future, too, the peoples of socialist countries and all the progressive people of the world, including the Asian, African and Latin American peoples, will render active support to the just struggle of our people for the peaceful reunification of the fatherland. They will deal a collective blow at the wild ambition of the imperialists to split our nation, a single nation, into two parts for ever, and their stooge's treachery to the country and nation.

The Algerian Democratic and People's Republic has made

positive efforts for the victory of the righteous struggle of our people in the international arena, always regarding our cause as its own, and, especially, extended great support to us at the Summit Conference of Non-Aligned States and the 28th Session of the United Nations General Assembly.

Our people will always remember this.

Allow me to take this opportunity to express once again deep thanks to His Excellency Mr. President Houari Boumedienne and the Algerian Government and people for the unstinted support and encouragement they extend to the policy of our Party and the Government of our Republic for the independent and peaceful reunification of the country and the struggle of our people for its implementation.

Speech at the Banquet in Honor of Prince Norodom Sihanouk, Head of State of Cambodia and Chairman of the National United Front of Kampuchea and Madam Princess Monique Sihanouk on April 12, 1974 (Excerpt)

Today big obstacles are still lying in the way of the independent and peaceful reunification of our country owing to the machinations of U.S. imperialism and its stooges to provoke war and perpetuate national split. But the situation as a whole keeps developing in our favor and to the disadvantage of the enemy.

In an attempt to save themselves from their catastrophic crisis, the U.S. imperialists and the south Korean authorities are further intensifying their fascist repression of the south Korean people and deliberately aggravating the tension between north and south, raising noisy "anti-communist" clamors.

This is, however, a foolish act from which they will get nothing.

The recent new proposal advanced by the Supreme People's Assembly of our country to conclude a peace agreement between our Republic and the United States clearly proves that we are making sincere efforts at all times for the peaceful solution of the Korean question.

If the United States, as a signatory to the Korean Armistice Agreement, is really interested in the peaceful settlement of the Korean question, it should naturally accept our peaceful initiative.

If the United States does not want to have direct talks with our Republic, it would be all right with us but only if it stops all forms of interference in the internal affairs of our country and withdraws its troops from south Korea, thereby opening a way for the Koreans to independently solve the reunification question for themselves.

If the U.S. government persist in its present attitude, rejecting both this and that proposal, it will bring only greater setbacks upon itself.

In order to realize the national aspiration for the peaceful reunification of the country, the people in the northern half of the Republic are vigorously pushing ahead with great socialist constructions, holding aloft the line of our Party. At the same time the student youth and people in south Korea have valiantly turned out in struggle against fascism and for democracy.

The Korean people will surely accomplish the cause of the country's peaceful reunification with an ever increasing support and encouragement of the peace-loving countries and peoples across the whole world.

Answers to the Questions Raised By the Chief Editor of Al Sahafa, Organ of the Sudanese Government

April 25, 1974

A llow me first to express my thanks to you for disseminating our Party's Juche idea through *Al Sahafa* and actively supporting our people's revolutionary struggle for national reunification and socialist construction.

Now let me answer your questions.

You asked us whether we were convinced of our victory from the first days of our struggle against the Japanese imperialist aggressors.

From our childhood we witnessed the miserable plight of our people downtrodden by the Japanese imperialist aggressors and experienced an acute sorrow as a stateless nation.

Occupying Korea, Japanese imperialism established a most brutal and tyrannical colonial rule over our country. The Japanese imperialist aggressors robbed our country of its wealth and ruthlessly exploited our people. They wantonly trampled underfoot even our people's elementary right to live and cruelly suppressed their struggle for freedom and liberation. The bestial, outrageous aggressors of Japanese imperialism massacred our patriots and plunged the whole country into a sea of blood.

We could not just look on the bestialities perpetrated by the burglarious aggressors of Japanese imperialism and the tragic lot of our fellow countrymen who, deprived of their nation, were going in rags and hungry, maltreated and humiliated. We started our struggle with a firm determination to crush the Japanese imperialist aggressors and regain our lost homeland at all costs and save our people from distress.

Of course, we never thought that we could easily defeat the ferocious aggressors of Japanese imperialism armed to the teeth. However, from the first days of our struggle, we were deeply convinced that we could certainly defeat them and achieve the independence of the country.

We firmly believed that we would surely win, because our revolutionary cause for the people's freedom and liberation against foreign aggressors was a just one. Human history shows that the just struggle of the oppressed masses of people against exploitation and repression and for freedom and liberation is sure to win. It is a law of historical development that the aggressors and oppressors go to ruin and the popular masses emerge victorious.

From the first days of our struggle we were convinced that the master of the Korean revolution is the Korean people and, therefore, the Korean people must and can shape their destiny only by their own efforts. It was our firm creed that when the popular masses are awakened to revolutionary consciousness and closely united they can display a really great force and defeat the aggressors with their own strength in whatever unfavorable and difficult conditions and win freedom and liberation.

Our struggle against the Japanese imperialist aggressors was indescribably hard. With a firm conviction of victory, however, we vigorously waged the struggle against the Japanese imperialist aggressors, revolutionally educating and closely uniting all those who loved the country and the people—workers, peasants, youths, students, religionists, traders and manufacturers—and thereby eventually destroyed Japanese imperialism and won national liberation.

Now, on your question as to how, in a very short period of history, we could get over the consequences of colonialism and build on the debris of war an economic foundation that could meet all our domestic demands.

A dependent and very backward economy handicapped by colonial lopsidedness was handed down to our people from the old society and even this was totally destroyed in the three-year war. Under the correct leadership of the Workers' Party of Korea, our people successfully carried out the postwar rehabilitation of the national economy in a little more than three years by displaying a high degree of creative enthusiasm and patriotic devotion and brilliantly accomplished the historic task of socialist industrialization in a very brief span of time—only 14 years—through an uninterrupted dynamic struggle. As a result, our country, once a backward colonial agricultural state, has now turned into a socialist industrial state with a powerful heavy industry, a modern light industry and a developed agriculture, which can build up the people's lives and manage the economy on its own.

This great victory won by our country is the fruit of the dedicated struggle waged by the entire people to carry through the Party's line for the building of an independent national economy by giving full play to their revolutionary spirit of self-reliance . . . Next, let me explain the reason why we oppose the admission of "two Koreas" to the UN.

As you know, at the UN General Assembly last year, US imperialism and its followers tabled a proposal for simultaneous entry of "two Koreas" into the UN. This proposal was a product of the "two Koreas" policy which had long been pursued by the US imperialists. When they failed to materialize their wild design to swallow up the whole of Korea by invading the northern half of the Republic, the US imperialists came out with the "two Koreas" policy for the purpose of keeping our country divided in two forever, and maintaining south Korea at least as their military base of aggression and commodity market. The south Korean authorities are zealously following the "two Koreas" policy of the US imperialists to retain even for a few more days their military fascist regime which is shaking to its very foundation.

We can never accept the proposal of the US imperialists and

their stooges for the simultaneous entry of "two Koreas" into the UN. If the north and south enter the UN separately before reunification, our country will remain divided forever. This is entirely counter to our people's will and desire. The permanent division of the country will spell immeasurable misfortunes and sufferings to our people and place a great obstacle to the future development of our nation.

Our people, who have lived as a homogeneous nation with one culture and one language for ages, do not want the split of the nation. They only want reunification. If there are any people in our country who oppose national reunification and want division, they are tiny handful of persons in authority, landlords and comprador capitalists in south Korea.

Ever since the country was partitioned into north and south, because of the occupation of south Korea by the US imperialist aggression army, we have exerted strenuous efforts to reunify the country independently by peaceful means. Last year when the divisive manoeuvres of the splitters within and without became more undisguised, we declared that the north and south must not enter the UN separately. If they are to enter it before the country is reunified, they should do as a single state under the single national title of the Confederal Republic of Koryo, at least after a confederation is set up.

The sincere efforts of the Government of the Democratic People's Republic of Korea to achieve the independent and peaceful reunification of the country, and our policy for the entry into the UN as a single state, have won unreserved support from the progressive people the world over. Last year the UN General Assembly actively supported our three principles of national reunification, the keynote of which is independence, peaceful reunification and great national unity. Thanks to the positive efforts of the representatives of many countries, including the Sudan, it adopted a resolution on the immediate dissolution of the "United Nations Commission for the Unification and Rehabilitation of Korea," a body on the US imperialist payroll and their tool of interference in our internal affairs. They completely checked and frustrated the plot for the admission of "two Koreas" to the UN woven by the US imperialists and their lackeys. This again proved clearly that our firm, consistent policy for the independent and peaceful reunification of the country is entirely correct.

At the Third Session of the Fifth Supreme People's Assembly held some time ago, the Government of our Republic took another initiative to create favorable prerequisites for the achievement of the independent and peaceful reunification of the country.

In our letter sent to US Congress in the name of the Supreme People's Assembly, we proposed talks on the question of concluding a peace agreement with the United States which, among other things, will stipulate that both sides shall not invade the other side and shall discontinue arms reinforcement and the arms race, that the United States shall not meddle in Korea's internal affairs or obstruct its reunification and shall withdraw their troops occupying south Korea, and that our country shall not be made a military base or operational base of any foreign country after the withdrawal of US troops.

In order to remove the tension between the north and the south and accelerate our country's independent and peaceful reunification, it is necessary today to replace the Armistice Agreement with a durable peace agreement. The Government of the Republic has made tireless efforts for the solution of this question and held dialogues with the south Korean authorities. However, they have not accepted any of our reasonable proposals but further intensified war preparations and divisive manoeuvres with US imperialist backing.

Facts show that the south Korean authorities have neither intention nor capacity to solve the question of concluding a peace agreement. In this situation we consider that it is most appropriate to discuss this question directly with the United States, a signatory to the Korean Armistice Agreement and the real power that is capable of guaranteeing a peace agreement.

The reasonable step we took at the recent session of the Supreme People's Assembly is warmly welcomed and supported by many countries and progressive people of the world. However, the US authorities have not yet shown any positive reaction. If they eventually turn down our just proposal, they will clearly reaffirm to the world that US imperialism is the most shameless aggressor who violates our people's sovereignty, hampers Korean reunification, and is the heinous enemy of peace.

As in the past so in the future, the Government of our Republic will strengthen solidarity with the socialist countries, countries of the third world and progressive people the world over. With their active support and encouragement we will carry on a tireless struggle to materialize the independent and peaceful reunification of our country.

I take this opportunity to express my deep gratitude to the Sudanese Government and people for their active support and encouragement to our Party's policy of independent and peaceful reunification and the Korean people's struggle for its implementation.